ANSWERING ISLAM

A CHRISTIAN RESPONSE TO THE CLAIMS OF ISLAM

ردًا على الإسلام:
رد مسيحي على
مزاعم الإسلام

A. YOUSEF AL-KATIB

LOGOS LIGHT

Answering Islam:
A Christian Response to the Claims of Islam

ISBN (13) (Paperback): 978-1-68109-099-3
ISBN (10) (Paperback): 1-68109-099-6
ISBN (13) (eBook): 978-1-68109-100-6
ISBN (10) (eBook): 1-68109-100-3

LogosLight™
an imprint of TellerBooks™
TellerBooks.com/LogosLight

t TellerBooks

www.TellerBooks.com

Manufactured in the U.S.A.

NOTE: Unless otherwise stated, all biblical Scriptures quoted herein are taken from the New King James Version. In some instances, the author uses the American Standard Version translation. In cases where the author discusses texts that in turn quote from the Bible, the translation used in the quoted text is used herein.

Contents

About the Imprint

The LogosLight™ imprint first started with the collection The Church Fathers Speak, a compilation of the voices of the early Church fathers and their teachings on sanctity and Christ-like living. This ancient wisdom guides the reader on the path to cultivating holiness that yields self-dominion, patience, and virtue.

LogosLight™ has since grown to encompass Christian poetry and inspirational books, translations of the Bible and Hebrew Scriptures, and various Christian records and Liturgies.

LogosLight™ books also examine the role of Judeo-Christian thought on the formation of Western civic institutions, the moral foundations of just societies, and the role of faith in civil governance.

LOGOS LIGHT

Abbreviations

English Translations of the Bible:

ASV ....American Standard Version
BBE................Bible in Basic English
Darby..............Darby Bible
ESV ....English Standard Version
ISV ....International Standard Version
KJV ....King James Version
MKJV.............Modern King James Version
NIV ....New International Version
NKJV ....New King James Version
RSV................Revised Standard Version

Books of the Bible:
1Ch.................Chronicles
1Co.................1 Corinthians
1Jn..................1 John
1Ki..................1 Kings
1Pe.................1 Peter
1Sa..................1 Samuel
1Th ....1 Thessalonians
1Ti..................1 Timothy
2Ch.................2 Chronicles
2Co ....2 Corinthians
2Jn ....2 John
2Ki..................2 Kings
2Pe..................2 Peter
2Sa..................2 Samuel
2Th ....2 Thessalonians
2Ti ....2 Timothy
3Jo ....3 John
Acts ....Book of Acts
Amos..............Book of Amos
Col..................Colossians
Dan.................Daniel
Deu.................Deuteronomy
Ecc..................Ecclesiastes
Eph ....Ephesians

Est ....Esther
Exo ....Exodus
Eze................Ezekiel
Ezr ....Book of Ezra
Gal................Galatians
Gen................Genesis
Hab................Habakkuk
Hag................Haggai
Heb................Hebrews
Hos ....Hosea
Isa................Isaiah
Jas................James
Jer................Jeremiah
Job ....Book of Job
Joel ....Book of Joel
John................Gospel of John
Jon ....Jonah
Jos ....Joshua
Jude ....Book of Jude
Jdg................Judges
Lam ....Lamentations
Lev ....Leviticus
Luke ....Gospel of Luke
Mal ....Malachi
Mark................Gospel of Mark
Mat ....Gospel of Matthew
Mic ....Micah
Nah................Nahum
Neh................Nehemiah
Num................Numbers
Oba................Obadiah
Phm ....Philemon
Php ....Philippians
Pro................Proverbs
Psa................Psalms
Rev ....Revelation
Rom................Romans
Ruth................Book of Ruth
Son ....Song of Solomon
Tit................Titus

Zec..................Zechariah
Zep ....Zephaniah

CHAPTER 1. INTRODUCTION

This book is not an attempt to prove the truth of the Bible. Rather, it is an attempt to show the reader that the claims that Islam makes about Christianity have logical and reasonable answers. It is to present a defense of Christianity and demonstrate to the Muslim or to the person considering conversion to Islam that Islam's claims against Christianity are not the last word. In many cases, the claims are based on flawed reasoning. In other cases, Christianity offers a sold rebuttal. This book sets forth Christianity's answers to the claims of Islam.

I. About the Author

In December of 1998, I experienced God. It was the most profound, powerful experience of my life. In the moments before I had this divine encounter, I found myself in a state of abysmal darkness. I had spiraled downward into hopelessness and despair. I believed I had discovered the ultimate meaningless of everything in the universe. I was entrenched in the hopeless worldview that the meaning we live by, whether religious, philosophical or cultural, is arbitrarily constructed by our minds. I descended into a deep state of hopelessness in that I believed, in those moments, that I had pierced the façade by which everyone else was deceived, and that by seeing the true hopelessness of everything, I would never again be able to relate to or commune with others.

Then Jesus came. On the night of 23 December 1998, he shattered my worldview like a stone shatters a fragile glass window. He demolished my idle, barren thinking and brought me hope and peace that I never thought possible. Through divine guidance, I was led to know that Jesus Christ is the light that illuminates darkness, the hope that disperses fear and the life that conquers death. From that encounter with Jesus of Nazareth, I came to know that everything I had been living for—prestige, approval, honor—were meaningless constructs, but Jesus Christ, the cornerstone of the Christian faith, is the ultimate meaning of everything ever created in the universe. He was not merely a prophet or the harbinger of a message, He was the message. He is the way, the truth and the life.

What I learned on the night of 23 December 1998, a night that forever changed my life, is that God had a great purpose for my life, and that by dying to myself and being reborn, I could escape my impending judgment and find new life. In those moments, I believed, and I accepted Jesus as my Lord and Savior. As I believed, all of the chaos of my idle thinking dissipated, and my mind was restored. I found a new life. It was as though a dark sheet that previously covered my eyes was pierced and torn asunder. I found peace. I became a disciple of Christ.

I cannot offer the reader any logical arguments to prove that Jesus Christ is Lord, nor can I offer the reader proof that my encounter with Christ in December of 1998 was real, that I am not making it up, that it was not a hallucination, that I am not crazy. Yet, what I can prove to the reader is that my life changed dramatically after that fateful night. The old me was gone and the new me was reborn. My life was filled with a new purpose, radiated by hope, faith and victory over sin and addiction in my life. Jesus transformed my life just as He transformed the lives of countless other sinners who sought to know the true God, the God of Abraham, Isaac and Jacob.

II. The Purpose of This Book

My encounter with Jesus in 1998 was deeply personal, and it cannot serve as a basis for the faith of any person other than me. To come to know Jesus as your Lord and Savior, you must encounter Him for yourself. It is my sincerely held belief that you can encounter Him. You must simply pursue Him. You must seek Him. And you must do so relentlessly, through persistent prayer. If you do, He will reveal Himself to you, and you will be compelled to believe that He is all that He claims to be in the Bible—the Christ, the Son of the living God.

Yet there is a second side to faith in Christ. It involves human reason. One may choose to believe in Christ as his or her savior and in the Bible as the word of God, but is such faith rational? Is it reasonable? Islam claims that it is not; it claims that the Bible is a corruption of the true word of God, that Christ was no more than a prophet and that God can have no son and no equal. Therefore, for the devout Muslim, Christianity is a perversion of the true faith, and faith in Christ contradicts the dictates of reason and the precepts of the true faith, as found in the Qur'ān and taught in Islam.

For 1,400 years, Islam has claimed that Christianity is a corruption of Islam, the one true religion. This book sets forth reasoned responses to Islam's claims. The purpose of this book is to show that for every claim made in Islam, there is a reasoned counterclaim in support of Christianity. This book acknowledges that the seeker who sets out to understand and know God through reason alone can never come to truly know God; reasoned arguments can be leveraged both in support of and against the tenets of Christianity. Ultimately, one cannot rely on logic, reason or science alone to either prove or disprove Christianity or the veracity of the Bible. Faith must fill the gap. Every seeker of God must make a choice to either accept the claims of Christ and the Bible or to reject them. Both choices involve faith. This book, by offering reasoned responses to Islam's claims against Christianity, demonstrates that the choice to follow Christ is not an unreasonable one. It is a choice that is supported by rational arguments. This book is an invitation to every Muslim to carefully weigh the arguments in favor of Christ and the claims of the Bible and, after considering the arguments and through careful prayer, to choose to accept Christ as Lord and Savior, and thereby experience new life, hope and eternal salvation.

CHAPTER 2. RESPONSES TO ISLAM'S ARGUMENTS: H. M. BAAGIL'S CLAIMS

I. Introduction

A. The Attack

In this section, I examine Dr. H. M. Baagil's *Muslim Christian Dialogue*, a treatise that sets forth a dialogue between a Christian seeking truth and a Muslim trying to guide the Christian towards the "light" of Islam. Through this section of the book, page references refer to pages in Dr. Baagil's treatise.

Muslim Christian Dialogue begins with the Muslim and Christian each defending his respective faith, but the Christian eventually gives in to the Muslim's arguments, concludes that the Bible has been corrupted and confesses that "There is no God but Allah and Muhammad is His Prophet." The book concludes with arguments attempting to prove not only that Muhammad is mentioned in the Bible, but that the Bible prophecies his coming.

In proselytizing against Christianity, Dr. Baagil's tract sets forth Islam's primary charges against Christianity: the corruption of Scriptures revealed to earlier prophets and the adoption of false and idolatrous doctrine. Dr. Baagil's treatise has been used by countless Islamic organizations to urge Christians to return to the pure, authentic, uncorrupted religion of Islam.

Yet Dr. Baagil's tract is flawed in numerous respects. It employs insidious and subtle twists of logic to support its conclusions and includes countless self-contradictions, false statements, circular arguments, illogicisms and erroneous biblical interpretations, in addition to employing the character of a truly obtuse Christian to engage in the dialogue. This Christian, who knows virtually nothing about the Christian Scriptures or orthodox Christianity, is unable to defend Christian doctrine before the Muslim and is so poorly versed that at one point, he even confuses the Holy Ghost and the angel Gabriel (p. 31).

The book is especially dangerous to the Christian or Muslim unschooled in Christian doctrine or having shallow biblical knowledge. Such a reader will fall prey to Dr. Baagil's traps, thus being led astray from the truth of the Gospel to an impotent form of religion that denies Jesus' salvific power.

B. The Rebuttal

At last—there is now an answer to Dr. Baagil's treatise. In this volume, A. Yousef Al-Katib sets forth a systemic reply to each of Dr. Baagil's attacks on Christianity. A. Yousef Al-Katib, himself a Christian convert who spent more than five years in religious study before experiencing the miraculous power of Jesus to heal and to save, thoroughly replies to, refutes and rebuts each of Dr. Baagil's arguments on a detailed point-by-point basis. He reveals Dr. Baagil's innumerable self-contradictions, false statements, historical inaccuracies, circular arguments and flawed biblical interpretations.

The purpose of this booklet is to reply to, refute and rebut the false statements set forth in Dr. Baagil's book and to prevent Christians from going astray in their faith. This booklet is also aimed towards Muslims, many of whom will inevitably share many of Dr. Baagil's false beliefs about Christianity, the Scriptures, God's grace, and the promise of salvation through Jesus. This book seeks to set Muslims free of the errors so commonly propagated in Islam about Christianity and to set the record straight by demonstrating to readers the many errors in Dr. Baagil's reasoning, historical account and biblical interpretation. In this way, this book seeks to guide the reader to the light of Christ the Savior, Messiah and Son of God.

II. Are the Hebrew and Christian Scriptures Corrupted? The Circular Reasoning of Islam

A. Overview

As we will see throughout this book, Muslim apologists take a two-prong approach to dealing with the Hebrew and Christian Scriptures.

- On the one hand, they argue that Muhammad's revelation of that revealed to all of the Jewish prophets and Jesus, who preceded him, so much so that a great deal of Islamic proselytism and tracts rely on the Hebrew and Christian Scriptures to attempt to draw from them prophesies of

Muhammad's coming. Some argue, for example, that the Holy Spirit referenced in the Scriptures is actually Muhammad.

- This approach, of course, leads to one obvious problem: The message of Muhammad contradicts the unified, harmonious message of Jesus and the Jewish prophets. Muslims respond to this by arguing that while Jesus and the prophets preached a message in accordance with that of Muhammad, the Jews and the Church corrupted this message, leaving us with the Bible that Jews and Christians around the world today use in prayer, study and worship.

B. Circular Argument

The problem with Islam's argument is that it is based on circular reasoning that is impossible to contradict. If the Christian states that the Qur'an cannot be the Word of God because it contradicts the Hebrew and Christian Scriptures, the Muslim replies that the Christian and Hebrew Scriptures have been corrupted. Yet if this is true, then why does the Muslim reference those same supposedly "corrupt" Scriptures when trying to prove that Muhammad was a prophet?

C. Refuting Islam's Arguments Based on the Christian Scriptures

Though Islam's arguments for Muhammad's vocation as a prophet are based on circular reasoning, the Christian should not be threatened by these arguments because, as we will see in this book, they are easily refuted.

III. Defenses against Claims

A. Contradictions, False Statements and Errors of Logic

1. Contradictions

a. *Is "Christianity" Mentioned in the Bible?*

Dr. Baagil's contradictions begin early on in his work. First, he says that Christianity is not mentioned in the Bible: "Neither the name Judaism nor Christianity is found in the Bible, not even in a Bible dictionary" (p. 10). But then he says that it is mentioned: "The word Christianity is mentioned only three times in the New Testament and first in Antioch" (p. 10).

b.   Was Judah a Jew?

At first, Dr. Baagil says "yes": "Judah was nicknamed 'Jew' so that only Judah's descendants were called Jews originally" (p. 13). However, the author later states indirectly that Judah was not a Jew, since the *Qur'an* states "Or say you that Abraham, Ishmael, Isaac, Jacob and the twelve sons of Jacob were Jews or Christians?" (2:140). The author uses this to suggest that the twelve sons of Jacob were not Jews. However, this appears to contradict his earlier statement, which is that Judah, one of the twelve sons of Jacob, was nicknamed "Jew." Why would Jacob be nicknamed "Jew" if he were not a Jew?

It is possible that the author would concede that Sura 2:140 does not negate that Judah was Jew. The *ayah* only asks a question without actually answering it. Rather, it goes on to simply state "Say: Do you know better or God? And who is more unjust than he who conceals a testimony that he has from God? And God is not heedless of what you do." It is therefore possible that *Allah* was asking whether Judah was a Christian or a Jew, without stating that he was neither.

However, this is not the author's interpretation of the *ayah*, since he uses it to support the argument that none of the Patriarchs were Jews.

c.   God cannot be Seen

Dr. Baagil argues that there is a contradiction between John 5:37, which states that "the Father Himself, who sent Me, has testified of Me. You have neither heard His voice at any time, nor seen His form," and John 14:9, where Jesus states, "He who has seen Me has seen the Father." This seeming contradiction is resolved below (see "Seeming Contradictions in Historical Narration," *infra.*), but for now, I wish to point out the Dr. Baagil's internal inconsistency.

On page 24, Dr. Baagil juxtaposes the two Scriptures in an attempt to argue that the Bible contradicts itself and is therefore corrupt. Then, on page 30, Dr. Baagil argues that what Jesus *really* means in John 14:9 ("He who has seen Me has seen the Father") is not that Jesus is God, but rather, that one "should believe in God by admiring his creation: the sun, the moon, all creation, and Jesus himself who was created by God" (p. 30).

When bolstering the argument that Jesus contradicts Himself when He states "you have not seen God's form," the author conveniently interprets Jesus to state John 14:9 that He and God are one; but when bolstering the argument that God can only be seen by looking at God's creation, Dr. Baagil conveniently switches interpretations and argues that Jesus in John 14:9 is stating that he who has seen Jesus or any other part of God's creation has seen evidence of God.

2. False Statements

a. Jesus Never Claimed to Be God

Muhammad A. Nubee's introduction states that "in the Bible Jesus (PBUH) never claimed to be God" (p. 3). While it may be true that in the Bible, Jesus never directly claimed to be God, in various places he indirectly claims to be God. Jesus states, for example:

- "I and the Father am one" (John 10:30).
- "If I am not doing the works of my Father, then do not believe me; but if I do them, even though you do not believe me, believe the works, that you may know and understand that the Father is in me and I am in the Father" (John 10:37-38).
- "Very truly I tell you, the Son can do nothing on his own, but only what he sees the Father doing; for whatever the Father does, the Son does likewise" (John 5:19).

Moreover, Jesus claimed the divine name for Himself. He said to the Jews: "I tell you the truth. Before Abraham was born I AM" ('John 8:58). The name "I AM" is the name God called Himself in Exo 3:14. The Jews understood that Jesus was calling Himself by the divine name, which is why they took up stones to stone him (John 8:59), which is in accordance with the Old Testament punishment for blasphemy (death by stoning) (Lev 24:16).

b. God Sent Prophets to Each Nation

Dr. Baagil asserts that "God sent to *each nation* a Prophet as a Warner, and some of them with a Scripture as a guidance for that particular nation only. The *Suhuf* to Abraham, the *Torah* (part of the Old Testament) to Moses, the *Zabur* (Psalms) to David, and the *Injeel* (New Testament) to Jesus" (p. 26) (italics added).

The problem with this account is that Dr. Baagil fails to recognize that the prophets that he cites, Abraham, Moses, David and Jesus, were all from the same nation: the nation of Israel. All of these prophets were from the seed of Jacob and preached to the people of Israel. God did not send, for example, a prophet to China, a prophet to Mali, a prophet to South America, etc. God sent prophets through Israel, choosing Israel as a "model community" to show the world his path. He used Israel to bless the world, as revealed in the vision of Jacob's ladder at Genesis 28:13-14: through Jacob's seed, all the families of the earth would be blessed.

To suggest, as does Dr. Baagil, that God sent prophets to "each" nation is inconsistent with the common histories of the prophets, since all of the prophets, including Moses, David and Jesus, were of the seed of Jacob and preached their messages primarily to the Israelites. Jesus was the only one of these who preached a message universal to all people, which, as described further below, Dr. Baagil also fails to understand.

c. *Jesus's Universal Gospel of Faith, Repentance and Salvation*

Dr. Baagil goes on to write that "Jesus himself said that he was sent only to the people of Israel (Matthew 15:24): 'I am not sent but unto the lost sheep of the house of Israel' (p. 26). Jesus here refers to his earthly ministry, which was directed to the Israelites, for since Abraham, Israel had been God's instrument for his message.

However, after Jesus' crucifixion and resurrection, a New Covenant was inaugurated that opened up the former Covenant to all people who would have faith and repent. Jesus' encounter with the Canaanite woman recounted by Dr. Baagil foreshadows this Covenant, for the woman's daughter was healed, even though the woman was a Canaanite (non-Jew), because she had faith (Mat 15:28).

This is made clear by Mark 16:15, where Jesus commands his disciples to "go into all the world, and preach the gospel to every creature." Dr. Baagil argues that "This contradicts what is mentioned above in Matthew 15:24 and Matthew 1:21 [Jesus shall "save his people from their sins"]. Secondly, Mark 16:9-20 has been expunged in many Bibles. The New American Standard Bible put this part in brackets and wrote the following commentary: 'Some of the oldest manuscripts omit from verse 9 through 20' ... This means also that the resurrection is not true as this is described in Mark 16:9" (p. 27).

First, while it is true that the earliest manuscripts and some other ancient witnesses do not contain Mark 16:9-20, this does not, as Dr. Baagil contends, mean that "the resurrection is not true as this is described in Mark 16:9" (p. 27). It simply means that in some of the oldest manuscripts of an ancient text nearly 2,000 years old, a portion of the text has been lost. It does not necessarily mean that the word and events of Mark 16:9-20 cannot be true. It may simply be that church scribes and leaders attempted to piece together the missing text from other fragments or by relying on the other Gospels, or simply that the earliest manuscripts matched later manuscripts, but fragments from the earliest manuscripts are missing.

In any case, the existence of the earliest manuscripts of Mark 16:9-20 is unnecessary because Jesus' commandment to preach the Gospel to every creature is reiterated in other Gospel accounts, namely Matthew ("Go ye therefore, and make disciples of all the nations, baptizing them into the name of the Father and of the Son and of the Holy Spirit" (Mat 28:19)) and Luke (Jesus said that "repentance and remission of sins should be preached in his name unto all the nations, beginning from Jerusalem" (Luke 24:47)).

That Jesus intended his message for all nations was made evident by the historical fact that Jesus' disciples traveled across Asia, Europe and Africa to spread his message among the Gentiles. His disciples understood that His message was a universal one for meant for all nations. So should we also understand this.

3. Circular Arguments

a. *The Bible is Corrupted when It Contradicts Muhammad, but it is God's Word when It Affirms Mohammed*

i. Overview

A fundamental problem with this book is that it claims that the Christian and Jewish sources are corrupt and therefore cannot be trusted, yet it constantly takes verses completely out of context and proclaims: "God's scripture points to Islam!" But either the Christian and Jewish sources are corrupted and should not be trusted at all or they should be wholeheartedly embraced as the Word of God. It is disingenuous to claim that they are false and then pick verses that one believes supports one's position.

ii. Examples

The farce of Dr. Baagil's position comes clearly to light when he quotes a Scripture to support one of his points, and yet the Scripture quoted simultaneously undermines another of his points. For example, on page 39, Dr. Baagil quotes a series of Scriptures to support his point that the doctrine of the Divine Sonship of Jesus and the Divinity of Jesus Christ are doctrines made by men (not God). He writes, that it is clear from Jesus' own sayings "that he never claimed divinity or identity to God: 'My Father is greater than I' (John 14:28); 'Father, into thy hands I comment my spirit' (Luke 23:46). 'But of that day and that hour knoweth no man, no, not the angels which are in heaven, neither the Son, but the Father' (Mark 13:32)" (p. 39). It would seem that, because Dr. Baagil quotes from these Scriptures, it must be these Scriptures must be parts of the Bible that were not corrupted. Otherwise, Dr. Baagil would argue against them rather than quote them to support his arguments. However, if these Scriptures are the true and uncorrupted words of Christ, then they prove rather than undermine the doctrine of the Sonship of Jesus. If Jesus were not the Son of God, He would not call God "Father" in all of these Scriptures.

Similarly, Dr. Baagil seeks to prove his point about the fact that Jesus and God the Father are not one by pointing to John 14:9, where Jesus asks Philip, "how can you say, 'Show us the Father'?" (John 14:9). Dr. Baagil's point is that by this phrase Jesus means that it is not possible for Jesus to show Philip the Father because unlike Jesus, who as incarnate, God is a spirit that no man has seen. Therefore, Jesus is distinct from the Father. We deal with this point as well as Dr. Baagil's convoluted interpretation of the Scripture and selective quoting thereof further below. For now, suffice it to say that Dr. Baagil's quotation of the Scripture in order to show that Jesus is not the Father undermines his argument about the Scriptures being corrupted. If they are corrupted, why then does he rely on them?

b. A Doctrine is True Because it is Stated in the Qur'an

One of the recurring problems in the book is that it bases the truth of certain statements on the fact that they appear in the *Qur'an*. This is problematic because the very purpose of the book is to prove the truth of the claims made in the *Qur'an*. Yet claiming the truth of a statement on the basis that it appears in the *Qur'an*, as where the author asserts that the name "Islam" was given by *Allah* Himself as mentioned in Sura 5:3 ("This day I have perfected your religion for you and completed My favor on you, and have chosen for you Islam as y our religion" (p. 10)), is based on a circular argument.

For example, Dr. Baagil writes that the contents of the *Qur'an* have been "guaranteed by *Allah* in *Surah* 2:2: 'This is the Scripture whereof there is no doubt ...' and also in *Surah* 15:9: 'No doubt we have sent down the *Qur'an* and surely We will guard it (from corruption)'" (p. 13). However, these assertions are based on the premise that the *Qur'an* is the true and uncorrupted word of God, a premise that is in dispute in the book.

4. Illogicisms and Conclusions Not Supported by Evidence Presented

a.   The Name "Christian" was First Given by Christians' Foes

The author writes that the word Christianity was first used in Antioch and later by King Agrippa II to Paul in Acts 26:28 ("Almost thou persuadest me to be a Christian") (p. 10). The author concludes that "the name Christian was first given by foes rather than friends" (p. 10). However, no evidence is given whatsoever that those who employed the name "Christian" in Antioch, where the name was first used, were the foes of Christians.

b.   Abraham the First to be Called Muslim

Dr. Baagil writes that the first to be called Muslim on earth "is not Muhammad but Abraham" (p. 10). However, no evidence whatsoever is offered to submit this claim or clarify who called Abraham. Was it Mohammed who first called Abraham a Muslim? Or did the companions of Abraham call him a Muslim? These questions remain unanswered.

c.   God Sent a Prophet to Each Nation

This is an argument that is particularly difficult to reconcile with the reality that all of the Hebrew and Christian prophets were in the line of Abraham through Isaac and Jacob. Dr. Baagil writes that "God sent to each nation a Prophet as a warner, and some of them with a Scripture as a guidance for that particular nation only. The *Suhuf* to Abraham, the Torah (part of the Old Testament) to Moses, the Zabur (Psalms) to David, and the Injeel (Gospel) to Jesus" (p. 26).

The problem here is that Moses, David and Jesus were all among and within the same nation: Israel! Only Abraham can be said to be "outside" of Israel, since technically speaking, Israel refers to the twelve tribes of Jacob, yet even Abraham is within the line of Israel's prophets. God never sent a biblical prophet from among the Arabs or other nations.

d. Pagan Influence Moved Sabbath Worship to Sunday

Dr. Baagil states that Roman paganism had influence in various Christian developments, including, for example, the Sabbath shift to Sunday (p. 29). He fails, however, to present any evidence in support of this. In contrast, some Christians believe the early church began meeting on Sundays soon after Christ rose from the dead, in honor of Christ's resurrection on Sunday, the first day of the week. This would be supported with Paul's injunction to meet together on the first day of the week (Sunday) to present offerings: "Now concerning the collection for the saints, as I have given orders to the churches of Galatia, so you must do also: On the first day of the week let each one of you lay something aside, storing up as he may prosper, that there be no collections when I come" (1Co 16:1-2).

B. Obtuse interpretations of the Scriptures

Another major problem with the book is the interpretations of verses in an obtuse manner that makes no sense and does not correspond to logic.

1. Abraham as "more an Arab than a Jew"

The author writes that "Abraham who was born in Ur of Chaldees could not have been a Jew. First because Ur of Chaldees was in Mesopotamia, which is now part of Iraq. He was then more an Arab than a Jew. Secondly the name Jew came after the existence of Judah, the great-grandson of Abraham" (p. 11).

This argument is flawed in several respects. First, the term "Jew" is not defined in the Bible as a "descendant of Judah." Nowhere is this implied or stated, nor is the term "Jew" defined in modern dictionaries as a "descendant of Judah." Rather, "Jew" is a loose term used in so many respects in modern English as generally encompass Jacob and all of his descendants. More broadly, it is used in the Bible to refer to one of faith, which would of course include Abraham. The Apostle Paul writes, "For he is not a Jew who is one outwardly, nor is circumcision that which is outward in the flesh; but he is a Jew who is one inwardly; and circumcision is that of the heart, in the Spirit, not in the letter; whose praise is not from men but from God" (Rom 2:28-29).

Therefore, Judaism is of the heart, not of outward circumstances, such as birth or geographical origin. Abraham is viewed throughout the Scriptures as the father of faith: "What then shall we say that Abraham our father has found according to the flesh? ... For what does the Scripture say? "Abraham believed God, and it was accounted to him for righteousness" (Rom 4:1, 4:3).

Therefore, Jews have been from all kinds of geographic origins throughout the Scriptures. Many were born in Egypt, for example, or even Babylon, yet this does not make them any less Jewish.

Dr. Baagil's argument is further flawed because the Old Testament never defines "Jew" or states that Abraham was or was not a Jew. Going back to the time of Abraham and Moses, no one was actually called a Jew; rather, they were called Hebrews, as in the case of Abraham (Gen 14:13).

Yet even if Dr. Baagil's argument was right, it does not prove anything. Whether the word "Jew" in the English language is used to encompass all those in covenant with God or only the descendants of Judah changes nothing in the Christian faith. One thing that is clear is that the Bible offers nothing to support Abraham as a Muslim who followed the teachings of Muhammad.

2. The "Burden upon Arabia" is not the Duty to Spread Islam, but a Judgment

For example, the book states, "Isaiah mentioned in chapter 21:13: 'the Burden upon Arabia,' which means the responsibility of the Muslim Arabs, of course of all Muslims now, to spread Islam" (p. 18). Actually the responsibility of the Muslim Arabs to spread the Islam is not at all mentioned, hinted or implied in Isaiah 21:13. Rather, the "burden" being referred to is punishment. The "burden" (or oracle) mentioned in the original Hebrew "often carries a message of doom" (note at Isa 13:1, *The NIV Study Bible*. See 21:1-9; 46:1-2; 47:1-15; Jer 50-51). *The NIV Study Bible* heads the section with "A Prophecy Against Arabia." The burden should thus be ready not a duty but as a condemnation.

3. The Holy Spirit was the Angel Gabriel

a. Overview

The next sample of Dr. Baagil poor biblical hermeneutics relates to that of Matthew 1:18 and Luke 1:26 and 27. Dr. Baagil interprets these verses to mean that the Holy Spirit is the angel Gabriel and by corollary, the angel Gabriel is a part of the Trinity.

Dr. Baagil writes:

> "Mu. Maybe the following questions will give you a better understanding of the Trinity: What is the Holy Spirit?
>
> "Cr. The Holy Spirit is the Holy Ghost, is also God. We are taught, the Father is God, the Son is God, the Holy Ghost is God. We are not allowed to say Three Gods, but One God.
>
> "Mu. Read Matthew 1:18.
>
> "Cr. "Now the birth of Jesus Christ was on this wise: When as his mother Mary was espoused to Joseph, before they came together, she was found with child of the Holy Ghost:"
>
> "Mu. Compare now with Luke 1:26 and 27.
>
> "Cr. "And in the sixth month the angel Gabriel was sent from God unto a city of Galilee, named Nazareth, To a virgin espoused to a man whose name was Joseph, of the house of David; and the virgin's name was Mary."
>
> "Mu. So in the miraculous birch of Jesus, Matthew mentioned the Holy Ghost and Luke mentioned the angel Gabriel. What is the Holy Ghost then?
>
> "Cr. The Holy Ghost is then the angel Gabriel.
>
> "Mu. Do you still believe in the Trinity now?
>
> "Cr. Then God is God, the Holy Ghost or the Holy Spirit is the angel Gabriel, and Jesus is ..." (p. 31).

The verses referenced by Dr. Baagil are as follow:

- "Now the birth of Jesus Christ was as follows: After His mother Mary was betrothed to Joseph, before they came together, she was found with child of the Holy Spirit" (Mat 1:18).
- "Now in the sixth month the angel Gabriel was sent by God to a city of Galilee named Nazareth, to a virgin betrothed to a man whose name was Joseph, of the house of David. The virgin's name was Mary" (Luke 1:26).

b. Dr. Baagil's Hermeneutical Problems

Dr. Baagil concludes that because Matthew states that Mary was with child by the Holy Spirit, and the angel Gabriel was sent by God to Mary, that the Holy Spirit must then be the angel Gabriel. However, while the Scripture is clear that Mary was with child by the Holy Spirit

(Mat 1:18), it never states that she was with child by the angel Gabriel or that the angel Gabriel was the Holy Spirit. Rather, it simply states that the angel Gabriel appeared to Mary to deliver to her the good news of the miraculous conception. The Evangelist of Luke writes:

> And having come in, the angel said to her, "Rejoice, highly favored one, the Lord is with you; blessed are you among women!" But when she saw him, she was troubled at his saying, and considered what manner of greeting this was. Then the angel said to her, "Do not be afraid, Mary, for you have found favor with God. And behold, you will conceive in your womb and bring forth a Son, and shall call His name JESUS (Luke 1:28-31).

If by this annunciation, we are to conclude that the angel Gabriel is the Holy Spirit, then by this logic if any woman is with child by her husband, and a postman is then sent to deliver a message to her, the postman must be the father of the woman's child. Of course, this is illogical and fallacious. There need be no relationship between one who delivers a message to a woman who the father of the woman's child.

In fact, the Gospel of Luke very clearly distinguishes between the Holy Spirit, by whom Jesus was conceived, and the angel Gabriel, sent by God to announce the good news:

> He will reign over the house of Jacob forever, and of His kingdom there will be no end." Then Mary said to the angel, "How can this be, since I do not know a man?" And the angel answered and said to her, "The Holy Spirit will come upon you, and the power of the Highest will overshadow you; therefore, also, that Holy One who is to be born will be called the Son of God (Luke 1:33-35).

It is important to note here that the angel Gabriel states that the "Holy Spirit will come upon you, and the power of the Highest will overshadow you" (Luke 1:35), *not* that he (Gabriel) would come upon her or overshadow her. Therefore, not only is there no evidence to suggest that the Holy Spirit is the angel Gabriel, as Dr. Baagil argues, but the testimony of the angel contradicts Dr. Baagil's argument.

4. Ishmael, Not Isaac, was Abraham's the Promised Son of the Covenant

Dr. Baagil writes that Ishmael rather than Isaac was Abraham's promised son of the Covenant and, furthermore, that it was Ishmael, not Isaac, whom Abraham was called to sacrifice. Dr. Baagil writes that "when the covenant [between Abraham and God] was made and sealed (circumcision and sacrifice) Abraham was ninety nine and Ishmael thirteen years old. Isaac was born a year later when Abraham was a hundred years old" (p. 52). The implication is that because Isaac was not yet born when the covenant was made and sealed, then he could not be the promised son.

Dr. Baagil's argument is flawed for the following reasons:

- In biblical covenants, including God's covenant with Abraham, God makes certain promises that He fulfills in the future, in exchange for certain behavior from his covenant people. The idea of promise is null if the action has already transpired. In other words, God would not have had to promised to Abram that he would he would have an heir who would come from his own body (Gen 15:4) and that Abram's descendants would be as numerous as the stars (Gen 15:5) if Abram already had an heir from his own body and his descendants were already as numerous as the stars.

- Even if the act promised had to have already been fulfilled at the birth of Isaac, as Dr. Baagil implies, then the fact that Isaac had not yet born when the covenant was made cannot serve as evidence that he is not the promised son because at the time that the covenant was made, Ishmael too had not yet been born. Rather, Ishmael was born later, out of desperation on the part of Sarai, who gave her maid Hagar to Abram to be Abram's wife and to conceive children (Gen 16:1-3).

- God later commanded circumcision of Abraham and all his male descendants as a sign of His covenant with Abraham (Gen 17:10). It is true that Ishmael was alive when God required this sign of the covenant and he was among those who were circumcised (Gen 17:23), but this does not prove that he was Abraham's promised son. All throughout Scripture, God makes covenants and seals them with signs before the thing promised comes to pass:

    o For example, Jesus promised a new covenant to His disciples and sealed it with the cup of the new covenant (Mat 26:27-28). The cup was a symbol of the new covenant to come about through the shedding of Jesus'

blood, which had not yet been shed at the time the
covenant was sealed at the last supper.

o   Similarly, God established a covenant with Noah, his
    sons, their descendants and every living thing that came
    out of the ark (Gen 9:8-10) whereby God would never
    again cut off all flesh through a flood (Gen 9:11). He
    set a rainbow in the clouds as a sign of the covenant
    (Gen 9:12-13). God's promise to never again destroy
    the earth through a flood was necessarily to be fulfilled
    after the covenant had been sealed through a rainbow.

o   In this same way, the circumcision was a sign of God's
    covenant with Abraham to make Abraham a great
    nation, with descendants as numerous as the stars (Gen
    15:5), which had not yet come to pass at the time the
    covenant was sealed.

-   If Dr. Baagil is correct in that a covenant is to be made and
    sealed after God's promise has already come to transpire, then
    what is to be made of the God's promise that Abraham's
    descendants would inherit land from the river of Egypt to the
    Euphrates (Gen 15:18)? This was part of God's covenant with
    Abraham, but it had not yet come to pass at the time God's
    covenant with Abraham was sealed at the circumcision of
    Genesis 17:10. Dr. Baagil's logic is problematic in that God's
    promise to give Abraham this land had not been realized, just
    as his promise to give Abraham and Sarah an heir, had not
    been realized at the time of the circumcision.

5. Jacob Performed Hajj

Dr. Baagil writes that a Christian "will shiver in hearing that
Pilgrimage or Hajj as is now done by Muslims by circumambulating
around the sacred stone Ka'bah in Mecca, had been performed by
many Prophets, even by Israelite Prophets" (p. 16). He then gives the
following example of Jacob:

> Gen 35:1 Then God said to Jacob, "Arise, go up to Bethel and dwell
> there; and make an altar there to God, who appeared to you when
> you fled from the face of Esau your brother."
> Gen 35:2 And Jacob said to his household and to all who were with
> him, "Put away the foreign gods that are among you, purify
> yourselves, and change your garments.

Gen 35:3 Then let us arise and go up to Bethel; and I will make an altar there to God, who answered me in the day of my distress and has been with me in the way which I have gone."
Gen 35:4 So they gave Jacob all the foreign gods which were in their hands, and the earrings which were in their ears; and Jacob hid them under the terebinth tree which was by Shechem.

From these Scriptures, Dr. Baagil concludes that Jacob performed Haj in Mecca and, just as Muhammad did, "removed all idols around the sacred stone Ka'bah in Mecca" (p. 16). There are several problems with this interpretation:

- Nowhere does it state in the Scripture that Bethel is Mecca. In fact, if you continue to read on, the Bible clearly states that Bethel is in the land of Canaan ("So Jacob came to Luz (that is, Bethel), which is in the land of Canaan, he and all the people who were with him" (Gen 35:6)). According to the biblical scholar and geographer Edward Robinson, ancient Bethel is modern day Beitin in Palestine, based on its fitting the location described in earlier texts, and on the philological similarities between the modern and ancient name, arguing that the replacement of the Hebrew el with the Arabic in was not unusual. Bethel was therefore in modern-day Israel, not modern-day Saudi Arabia.
- Nowhere does God instruct Jacob to perform a "pilgrimage";
- Nowhere is the Ka'bah stone mentioned.

6. Paul's Islamic Ablution

The author implies that Paul, a Muslim at the time of Jesus, undertook the Islamic ablution by "purifying" himself: "Acts 21:26 Then Paul took the men, and the next day, having been purified with them, entered the temple to announce the expiration of the days of purification, at which time an offering should be made for each one of them" (p. 15). This would imply that Paul, like Jesus and all the other Jews, were genuine Muslims, except that Paul later went astray and started preaching that Jesus was the Messiah and Son of God (or did he preach Muhammad with the Epistles later being forged?).

The reality is that ablution existed in both Judaism as well as in Islam. The fact that Paul "purified" himself does not indicate that the Paul followed Muhammad's teaching. Rather, he was following the teaching given by God to Moses:

Exo 30:17 Then the LORD spoke to Moses, saying:
Exo 30:18 "You shall also make a laver of bronze, with its base also of bronze, for washing. You shall put it between the tabernacle of meeting and the altar. And you shall put water in it,
Exo 30:19 for Aaron and his sons shall wash their hands and their feet in water from it.
Exo 30:20 When they go into the tabernacle of meeting, or when they come near the altar to minister, to burn an offering made by fire to the LORD, they shall wash with water, lest they die.
Exo 30:21 So they shall wash their hands and their feet, lest they die. And it shall be a statute forever to them--to him and his descendants throughout their generations."

Purification was thus required of Aaron and his sons when going into the tabernacle of meeting or nearing the altar. On this basis, Paul, as recounted by Dr. Baagil, purified himself before entering the temple (p. 15).

7. There are At Least Two Christian Gods

Dr. Baagil similarly misinterprets John 1:1 ("In the beginning was the Word, and the Word was with God, and the Word was God") by writing that there must be at least two Christian gods (p. 34). He fails to understand here that Jesus and the Father are one (John 10:30), not two separate gods.

From Isaiah 45:8 ("I, the LORD, have created [the heavens, the earth]"), Dr. Baagil concludes, "God alone was the Creator and no one else, not even Jesus, participated in the creation" (p. 34). Again, in this conclusion, he fundamentally misses and misinterprets the Christian doctrine that Jesus and the Father are on (John 10:30). This misunderstanding impedes Dr. Baagil from properly understanding how John 1:1 ("the Word [Jesus] was God") can be reconciled with 1 Timothy 2:5 ("For there is one God and one Mediator between God and men, the Man Christ Jesus").

8. Was Jesus Coequal to the Father?

a. Overview

One of the most difficult aspects of Christianity for a Muslim to accept is the idea that Jesus is both God and the Son of God. First, this strikes the Muslim as impossible: how could God be a man? God transcends creation and is omnipresent. He is not limited to physical form. Second, it strikes the Muslim as a contradiction: how could Jesus be both God and God's son? Third, it borders too closely to idolatry to the Muslim: because the Muslim cannot accept a man as God (or as God incarnate), the worship of Jesus as God is coequal to idolatry.

The various questions discussed above are treated throughout this discussion. At this time, however, we treat the points made by Dr. Baagil on page 30 of his treatise, where he seeks to undermine the Christian teaching that Jesus and God the Father are one.

b. Overview and Explanation of Dr. Baagil's Argument

Dr. Baagil writes:

> "Cr. But Jesus is God according to John 14:9: ". . . he that hath seen me hath seen the Father."
>
> "Mu. See to the context now, what is before and after this: John 14:8): "Philip saith unto him, Lord, shew us the Father, and it sufficeth us." (John 14:9): "Jesus saith unto him, have I been so long time with you, and yet hast thou not known me, Philip? he that hath seen me hast seen the Father; and how sayest thou then, Shew us the Father?"
>
> "So finally Jesus asked Philip how to show the appearance of God to the disciples, which is not possible. You should believe in God by admiring his creation: the sun, the moon, all creation, and Jesus himself who was created by God. He said (John 4:24): "God is a Spirit..." and (John 5:37): ". . . ye have neither heard his voice at any time, nor seen his shape." How can you see a spirit then? What they saw was Jesus and not God.
>
> "Also Paul said (I Timothy 6:16): '. . . whom no man hath seen, nor can see. . :' So what you can see is never God" (p. 30).

Dr. Baagil's point is therefore the following:

- When Philip said to Jesus to "show us the Father" (John 14:8), Jesus did not simply reply "He who has seen Me has seen the Father" (John 14:9); Jesus also added "so how can you say, 'Show us the Father'?" (John 14:9).
- According to Dr. Baagil, by this phrase Jesus means that it is not possible for Jesus to show Philip the Father and, by inference, that Jesus is not the Father because one can see Jesus but cannot see the Father. Therefore, Jesus is distinct from the Father.

- Dr. Baagil tries to bolster this interpretation by pointing to John 4:24 ("God is Spirit"); John 5:37 ("You have neither heard His voice at any time, nor seen His form"); and 1 Timothy 6:16 ("whom no man has seen or can see, to whom be honor and everlasting power").

We shall take each of Dr. Baagil's points in turn.

c. Weaknesses of Dr. Baagil's Interpretations

i. Jesus is God, but He is not the Father

The confusion first creeps in when the Christian, in trying to bolster the argument that Jesus is God, quotes John 14:9. The problem here is that John 14:9 does not, as the Christian hopes, support the thesis that Jesus is God. The Christian would have done much better to have cited any of the many verses that directly states that Jesus is God, such as John 1:1 ("In the beginning was the Word, and the Word was with God, and *the Word was God*"); Titus 2:13 ("our great *God* and Savior *Jesus Christ*"); or 1 John 5:20 ("we are in Him who is true, in His Son Jesus Christ. This is the true God and eternal life").

So what *does* John 14:9 say? It does *not* state that Jesus is God. Rather, it states that he who has seen Jesus "has seen the Father." Why? Because Jesus is "in the Father, and the Father in [Jesus]" (John 14:10). In other words, Jesus and the Father are *one in essence* (see John 10:30); they are each distinct persons in the Trinity who share the same nature. Therefore, anyone who sees Jesus sees the Father's essence. However, Jesus does not state that "I am the Father," but rather, "I am *in* the Father" (John 14:10) (italics added).

Rather, the Scriptures teach clearly that Jesus is distinct from the Father, though both Jesus and the Father are God. That the Father and Jesus are distinct persons is most clearly manifested at the baptism of Jesus, when the Father was manifested as the voice in heaven with the Son as Jesus below. The Father stated, "This is My beloved Son, in whom I am well pleased" (Mat 3:17). As clarified by 2 Peter 1:17, this voice was the voice of God the Father. The distinction of the two persons is made clear by the bodily form of the incarnate Son and the voice of God the Father descending from Heaven.

That Jesus is distinct from the Father is further clarified by the Great Commission, where Jesus instructed the disciples to "make disciples of all the nations, baptizing them in the name of the Father and of the Son and of the Holy Spirit" (Mat 28:19). If the Father and the Son were the same person, then mentioning both of them would have been redundant.

ii. Other Verses Cited by Dr. Baagil

So how, then, do we make sense of the verses that Dr. Baagil puts forward in support of the argument that it is impossible to see the Father (John 4:24 ("God is Spirit"); John 5:37 ("You have neither heard His voice at any time, nor seen His form"); and 1 Timothy 6:16 ("whom no man has seen or can see, to whom be honor and everlasting power")). We will deal with each verse in turn.

(1) "God is Spirit" (John 4:24)

The full verse is, "God is Spirit, and those who worship Him must worship in spirit and truth" (John 4:24). Jesus was speaking to the Samaritan woman and affirms that God is a spirit. While this is true, one must remember that the spirit of God is only one of the three persons of the Godhead. The Father and the Son are the other members of the Godhead. Because God chose incarnation as the vehicle for the atonement and salvation of mankind, Jesus the Son was visible, though the Holy Spirit is not visible. This is affirmed in John 1:18, which states, "No one has seen God at any time. The only begotten Son, who is in the bosom of the Father, He has declared Him." In other words, while no one has seen God, Jesus has made Him known. Jesus was in the form of God (Php 2:6) (*i.e.*, incapable of being seen), but took on the likeness of men (Php 2:7) so that God would be known (John 1:18).

(2) "You have neither heard His voice at any time, nor seen His form" (John 5:37)

This excerpt is found in the following words spoken by Jesus: "the Father Himself, who sent Me, has testified of Me. You have neither heard His voice at any time, nor seen His form" (John 5:37).

First, it is necessary to point out that Jesus is speaking to the Jews that persecuted him (see John 5:16). Second, we should emphasize what Jesus told his disciple Philip: "He who has seen Me has seen the Father" (John 14:9).

It would seem that there is a contradiction in the Gospel of John between 5:37, where Jesus states that the Jews had not seen the

Father's form (even though they saw Jesus) and 14:9, where Jesus said to Philip that "He who has seen Me has seen the Father" (John 14:9). However, there is actually no contradiction. The Greek word that Jesus uses in both verses is the same, and can be translated as "see." However, it has a secondary meaning that implies a deeper level of "seeing," one that involves knowledge and insight. It is this secondary meaning, which can be translated as "know" or "perceive," that Jesus is likely using, for the following reasons:

-   The Scriptures clearly state that He who sees God's face will die (Exo 33:20). For this reason, He only allows Moses to see His back (Exo 33:22-23) and, when He reveals Himself to other persons, he takes on a temporary form for the occasion (*e.g.*, the man with whom Jacob wrestled until dawn (Gen 32:24, 30) or the three men who visited Abraham (Gen 18:1-2)). Therefore, the term used by Jesus cannot be referring to "seeing" because then Philip and the others would, in "seeing" Jesus, see God the Father and die. He must then be referring to "knowing" Jesus.
-   The Jews that Jesus refers to in John 5:37 had not "seen His [God's] form." Jesus was the form that God took; the Pharisees could physically see Jesus, but they could not know or "perceive" that Jesus was the incarnate manifestation of God. The reason for this inability to know Jesus is explained in the following verse; it is "because whom He sent, Him you do not believe" (John 5:38).
-   It would be illogical if the word spoken by Jesus meant to "see" in the sense of perceiving by sight because Jesus is distinct from the Father (consider, *e.g.*, the reference to "the God and Father of our Lord Jesus Christ" (Eph 1:3), which distinguishes the Father and the Son). Thus, while Jesus and the Father are "one" (John 10:30), this unity refers to essential unity, not personal unity. Thus, it is not he who sees Jesus physically who sees the Father, but he who "knows" or "perceives" who Jesus is who then "knows" or "perceives" the Father (*i.e.*, the Father's essence).
-   Any other interpretation of John 5:37 would contradict John's earlier statement that "No one has ever seen God" (John 1:18).
-   In stating that "No one has seen God at any time. The only begotten Son, who is in the bosom of the Father, has made Him

known" (John 1:18), John distinguishes between seeing in the sense of physical perception and knowing. This distinction enables the reader to see how it is possible that while God has never been seen, He is able to be known in Christ. In other words, through Jesus, the Son of God, one is able to perceive the essence of God the Father.

(3) "Whom no man has seen or can see, to whom be honor and everlasting power" (1Ti 6:16)

The full verse references, "our Lord Jesus Christ's appearing, which He will manifest in His own time, He who is the blessed and only Potentate, the King of kings and Lord of lords, who alone has immortality, dwelling in unapproachable light, whom no man has seen or can see" (1Ti 6:14-16).

As with the previous verses ("no man shall see Me, and live" (Exo 33:20); "God is Spirit" (John 4:24); "No one has seen God at any time" (John 1:18)), this verse once again affirms that no man has seen God.

Some translations are somewhat ambiguous as to whether it is Jesus (as the Son of God) or God Himself who is being referred to. However, it should be clear that God is being referred to for the following reasons:

-   Certain translations make this clear. For example, the NIV states, "which God will bring about in his own time—God, the blessed and only Ruler, the King of kings and Lord of lords, who alone is immortal and who lives in approachable light, who no one has seen or can see" (1Ti 15-16).
-   It would not make sense if it were referring to Jesus because Jesus *was* seen—by the disciples, by the Pharisees, and by the multitudes.
-   The verse refers to the "King of kings" and "Lord of lords." God Himself is referred to as the Lord of lords in the Old Testament (Deu 10:17 and Psa 136:3). Jesus was only mentioned as the Lord of lords for the first time in Revelation (Rev 17:14), a book that scholars estimate was written approximately thirty years after 1 Timothy. It is likely that Paul meant the expression to refer to God in the same way that earlier references to "Lord of lords" referred to God, since there was no precedent marking otherwise.

- 1 Timothy 6:15 must be referring to God because it states that He will "bring about in his own time" the appearing of our Lord Jesus Christ. First, it would not make sense for Jesus to "bring about" His own appearing. Second, from other parts in the Bible, we know that only God the Father knows of Jesus' appearance; not even Jesus knows of the day ("But of that day and hour no one knows, not even the angels in heaven, nor the Son, but only the Father" (Mark 13:32)). If only the Father knows of the day, then only He can manifest it in His own time (1Ti 6:15). Accordingly, it is God the Father, not Jesus the Son, whom no man has seen.

C. Specific Topics Relating to Christian Doctrine

1. The Atonement as a Contradiction of the Biblical Teaching of Each Man Dying for His Own Sins

a. Dr. Baagil's Argument

Dr. Baagil argues that the Atonement contradicts various biblical verses teaching that each man dies for his own sin (p. 49). He points specifically to the following:

- "Fathers shall not be put to death for their children, nor shall children be put to death for their fathers; a person shall be put to death for his own sin" (Deu 24:16).
- "But every one shall die for his own iniquity; every man who eats the sour grapes, his teeth shall be set on edge" (Jer 31:30).
- "The soul who sins shall die" (Eze 18:4) ... "The soul who sins shall die. The son shall not bear the guilt of the father, nor the father bear the guilt of the son. The righteousness of the righteous shall be upon himself, and the wickedness of the wicked shall be upon himself" (Eze 18:20).

As an initial clarification, the Deuteronomy passage that Dr. Baagil cites is given to the Israelites as part of the Mosaic law. It applies not to God's judgment of man for man's iniquity, but rather, to the judicial punishments that the Israelites were to impose on sinners who broke God's law. The Israelites were not to put to death a person for his father's or children's sins. The Jeremiah and Ezekiel passages, in contrast, deal with general principles of justice. They state that God will judge a man based on his own righteous or wicked acts, and each man is ultimately accountable for his own actions.

b. Apparent Contradiction

The apparent contradiction is that, on the one hand, Jeremiah and Ezekiel affirm that God's judgment applies to each individual according to his own sins, not those of, for example, his father or child. A righteous person brings righteousness upon himself and a wicked person brings wickedness upon himself. One who acts righteously shall live (Eze 18:17) and one who does iniquity shall die (Eze 18:18).

Yet Jesus, who was innocent and without blemish (1Pe 1:19), died a sinner's death. Sinners, who deserve death (Rom 6:23), are given life through Jesus (John 3:16). If God's law in Jeremiah and Ezekiel is applied, then should not the sinner himself die, rather than have Jesus take his place on the cross?

c. Answer

God's law implements a system justice in which death is the consequence of sin (Rom 6:23). At the same time, God tempers His justice with grace, which is expressed through forgiveness. Under God's law, a sinner is to be put to death (Rom 6:23). Through His grace, God allows a sinner to substitute his death with that of an animal, offered to God as a sacrifice, as there is no forgiveness without the shedding of blood (Heb 9:22).

Animal sacrifice for sin atonement was established in the Mosaic law: Leviticus details the nature of the sacrifice that was to be made as an "atonement" to bring forgiveness of sin (Lev 4:33-35). Yet it may even go as far back as the Garden of Eden: God made for Adam and Eve "tunics of skin" (Gen 3:21), which implies that God put to death an animal, perhaps to cover not only Adam and Eve's shame, but also their sin.

Whereas the Israelites were able to experience God's forgiveness through animal sacrifice under His law, even for sins as serious as idolatry (Hos 14:3), other peoples, such as the Amelkites, were systematically wiped away for their sin (1Sa 15:1-3).

The crucifixion of Christ is then to be characterized as one final, perfect sacrifice (Heb 9:26), the realization of Old Testament substitute sacrifice for atonement. Animal sacrifices foreshadowed and mirrored Jesus' sacrifice on our behalf, but it was imperfect in that it required constant repetition and did not transform the sinner into a new creature.

In other words, to view the Atonement as a contradiction of Jeremiah and Ezekiel requires one to reach Jeremiah and Ezekiel in a vacuum, as reflections of God's justice while ignoring the countless examples in which God allowed mercy to substitute justice, beginning with the very first animal sacrifices that he permitted as substitutes for the death that sinners deserved. To truly understand the biblical text and context for the Atonement, one must read the Mosaic law together with the principles of justice promulgated by Jeremiah and Ezekiel and God's mercy, which frequently throughout the Scriptures, has tempered the strict application of the law.

2. The "Degrading" of Many "Prophets" in the Bible

Dr. Baagil goes on to devote an entire section of the book to the subject of "the degrading of many Prophets in the Bible as worshipers of false gods and accusing them of incest, rape and adultery" (p. 24). This section of the book is problematic in several respects. We will examine these issues first with a general overview and then by discussing each of Dr. Baagil's individual claims.

a. Overview

This section of the book is problematic in two main respects: (i) Dr. Baagil fails to understand the meaning of the word "prophet"; and (ii) Dr. Baagil fails to recognize the biblical concept of total depravity.

i. The Meaning of "Prophet"

The word "prophet" of course has several meanings, but all of these meanings have in common the act of predicting, forecasting or otherwise proclaiming the will of God:

(1) Narrow Definition: The Major and Minor Prophets

"Prophet" can be interpreted to mean the prophets Isaiah, Jeremiah, Ezekiel and Daniel (the major prophets) along with the twelve minor prophets (Hosea, Joel, Amos, Obadiah, Jonah, Micah, Nahum, Habbukah, Zephaniah, Haggai, Zechariah, Malachi) of the Old Testament. This is even one of the definitions given to "prophet" in the Oxford English dictionary ("Isaiah, Jeremiah, Ezekiel, Daniel, and the twelve minor prophets").

This definition would be too narrow for Dr. Baagil, since he includes in his definition of "prophet" biblical figures as diverse as David and Lot.

(2) Broader Definition

According to the Oxford English dictionary, a "prophecy" is defined as "a prediction" and "the faculty or practice of prophesying," which is in turn defined as predicting and speaking or writing "by divine inspiration." Therefore, predicting or forecasting is an integral part of prophesying.

Of course, this definition also would not suit Dr. Baagil, because many of those that he considers "prophets," such as Solomon or Lot, never predicted or forecast any event. For the benefit of Dr. Baagil, we shall search for a broader definition.

(3) Broadest Definition

The broadest definition of "prophet" in standard English usage is one of the first two alternative definitions given in the Oxford English dictionary, which defines a prophet as "a person regarded as an inspired teacher or proclaimer of the will of God." Therefore, teaching or proclaiming is an integral part of the definition.

Yet even with this definition, several of the individuals regarded by Dr. Baagil as prophets, including, for example, Lot, and Jacob, never taught or proclaimed anything.

(4) Conclusion

In conclusion, Dr. Baagil picks individuals in the Bible to impugn the righteousness of God's prophets without ever considering whether they bear any resemblance to prophets or to the act of prophesying. It seems in selecting his examples, he is simply picking among men whose sins were mentioned in the Bible. He then calls them prophets and impugns the validity of the Bible thereby. The only thing these men have in common is that the Bible depicts them at some points of their lives as righteous and in others as having sinned. This really does not tell us anything about the character of the true prophets of the Bible, such as Isaiah, Jeremiah, Daniel and Ezekiel.

ii. Total Depravity

Yet even if Dr. Baagil was able to point to the sins of the true prophets, those who heard Gods' will and then proclaimed it to their followers and taught it to the multitudes, it still means nothing. Unlike Islam, Christianity proclaims that "all have turned aside, They have together become corrupt; There is none who does good, No, not one" (Psa 14:3). Christians believe that even those given the gift of prophecy remain in a fallen state of sinfulness and are subject to all kinds of temptation and continue to fall after accepting Jesus as their savior. The fact that even a man given the gift of prophecy can fall into sin further strengthens the Christian doctrine of needing grace for salvation. If anything, it shows that one may live a life of sin and later encounter God, repent and receive the gift of prophecy, or, in contrast, one may have the gifts of the Holy Spirit and then relinquish them for a life of sin. Christianity never claimed that a man having the gift of prophecy (or any of the gifts of the Holy Spirit) could never be subject to sin in his life.

b. Individual Claims

i. Noah Drunk and Naked before his Sons

(1) Overview

Dr. Baagil writes, "Noah is shown to have been drunk to the point of becoming naked in the presence of his grown-up sons (Genesis 9:23-24): 'And Shem and Japhet took a garment, and laid it upon both their shoulders, and went backward and covered the nakedness of their father; and their faces were backward, and they saw not their father's nakedness. And Noah awoke from his wine, and knew what his younger son had done unto him'" (p. 24).

Following is a discussion of the problems with Dr. Baagil's argument.

(2) Noah was a "Righteous Man," not a Prophet

Noah was not a "prophet" in the full sense of the word. One may argue that Noah was a "prophet" because God revealed the future to him ("after seven days I will cause it to rain on the earth forty days and forty nights, and I will destroy from the face of the earth all living things that I have made" (Gen 7:4)), but this definition has no precedent in Christian doctrine. If anyone who has heard God's will can be deemed a prophet, then anybody who has ever received and read the Bible would be deemed a prophet! It would essentially mean erasing the very clear distinction the Bible makes when highlighting those special individuals that God calls to hear and proclaim his will, that is, the prophets.

(3) Noah was Generally a Righteous Man who is Mischaracterized by Dr. Baagil

We know that Noah was a "righteous" man (Gen 7:1), and this is why he was chosen by God. We also know that Noah became drunk and lay naked in his tent (Gen 9:21). We can reconcile this by concluding that while Noah was generally a righteous man, he sinned in becoming drunk this one time. From the context, it appears this was not habitual behavior. Rather, it is implied this was the first time Noah got drunk, since Noah only "began" to be a farmer *after* the flood and planted the vineyard (Gen 9:20), whose grapes evidently produced the wine from which he became drunk. We cannot judge a man's life and character on a single episode.

Dr. Baagil's characterization of Noah as having become "drunk to the point of becoming naked in the presence of his grown-up sons" is a mischaracterization. The reality is that Noah became drunk, and this was his sin. He was not parading about naked in front of his sons as a result of his drunkenness. Rather, he was laying passively naked in the privacy of his own tent (Gen 9:21) and was stumbled upon by his son Ham (Gen 9:22).

ii. King Solomon's Harem and Idolatry

(1) Overview

Dr. Baagil writes, "Solomon was accused not only of having a large harem but also of worshiping their false gods (I Kings 11:9-10): 'And the Lord was angry with Solomon ... And had commanded him concerning this thing, that he should not go after other gods: but he kept not that which the Lord commanded'" (p. 25).

Following is a discussion of the problems with Dr. Baagil's argument.

(2) Solomon was a King, was not a Prophet

It is of course true that Solomon was a man given the gift of wisdom by God. When the Queen of Sheba heard of the fame of Solomon and of his wisdom, she came to test him with hard questions (1Ki 10:1). She came to Jerusalem with camels that bore spices, gold, and precious stones (1Ki 10:2). He answered all her questions (1Ki 10:3) and when she had seen all his wisdom and prosperity (1Ki 10:4-5), she was amazed and proclaimed that it greatly exceeded what she had heard about Solomon (1Ki 10:6-7).

However, this gift of wisdom is different from the gift of prophecy given to prophets such as Isaiah, Jeremiah and Micah, who prophesied regarding a future covenant and proclaimed God's will to their people.

(3) Solomon's Sin is Recognized and Condemned in the Bible

The Bible is unequivocal with respect to Solomon's sin: both his love of women and his idolatry. The Bible teaches that King Solomon loved many foreign women, as well as the daughter of Pharaoh (1Ki 11:1). He loved women of whom the Lord said, "You shall not intermarry with them, nor they with you. Surely they will turn away your hearts after their gods" (1Ki 11:2). He had seven hundred wives, princesses, and three hundred concubines; and his wives turned his heart after other gods. As a result, Solomon's heart was not loyal to the Lord (1Ki 11:3-4).

Because of his marriage to women with foreign gods, Solomon built a high place for Chemosh, the god of Moab, and for Molech, the god of Ammon (1Ki 11:7). God became angry with Solomon (1Ki 11:9) and said to him, "Because you have done this, and have not kept My covenant and My statutes, which I have commanded you, I will surely tear the kingdom away from you and give it to your servant. Nevertheless I will not do it in your days, for the sake of your father David; I will tear it out of the hand of your son. However I will not tear away the whole kingdom; I will give one tribe to your son for the sake of my servant David, and for the sake of Jerusalem which I have chosen" (1Ki 11:11-13).

The story of Solomon is thus intended by God as instruction for what can happen when a man departs from the way of God. For Solomon, it was not a mere case of sin that could be set right through some repentance or offering atonement. As a result of Solomon's sin, God tore the entire northern kingdom from Solomon's son Rehoboam (1Ki 11-12). One can even argue that as a result of this split, a weakened Israel was able to be conquered by Assyria in the north and Babylon in the south. The sins of Solomon were thus destructive not only to himself (and possibly his own salvation), but to the entire kingdom of Israel.

iii. Aaron's Idolatry

(1) Overview

Dr. Baagil writes, "Aaron, as a Prophet who had accompanied his brother Moses to go to Pharaoh, was accused of having fashioned the golden calf for the Israelites to worship (Exodus 32:4): 'And he [Aaron] received them [golden earrings] at their hand, and fashioned it with a graving tool, after he had made it a golden calf: and they said, These be thy gods, O Israel, which brought thee up out of the land of Egypt'" (p. 25).

(2) Aaron was a Priest, not a Prophet

The central problem in Dr. Baagil's argument is that Aaron was thus a priest, not a prophet. God commanded Moses to take Moses' brother Aaron and his sons Nadab, Abihu, Eleazar, and Ithamar to minister to God as priests (Exo 28:1).

In fact, when Miriam and Aaron spoke against Moses and questioned whether God had spoken only through Moses and not through them also (Num 12:1), God's anger was aroused, implying that Aaron and Miriam were not prophets. Hearing Miriam and Aaron's murmur, God called them out and said, "if there is a prophet among you, I make Myself known to him in a vision; I speak to him in a dream" (Num 12:6). God was angered by the murmuring (Num 12:9) and Miriam became leprous as a result (Num 12:10).

Because Aaron was a priest and not a prophet, his sin was not a reflection of the sins of the prophets.

iv. Lot's Incest with his Two Daughters

(1) Overview

Dr. Baagil writes, "You will read of the incest of Prophet Lot with his two daughters (Genesis 19:36): 'Thus were both the daughters of Lot with child by their father'" (p. 25).

Following is a discussion of the problems with Dr. Baagil's argument.

(2) Lot was a Righteous Man, but not a Prophet

The biblical record attests to the fact that Lot was a righteous man. The Second Epistle of Peter states that "righteous Lot" was "oppressed by the filthy conduct of the wicked" (2Pe 2:7). However, nothing in the biblical record indicates that Lot was a prophet or that he taught or proclaimed any prophetic messages.

Of course, God communicated to Lot through angels who warned Lot to flee the city (Gen 19:12) and who took Lot, his wife and his two daughters by the hands to set them outside of the city (Gen 19:15-16). One of the angels told them not look back, lest they be destroyed (Gen 19:17).

This divine communication to Lot does not make Lot a prophet. Christians believe that God communicates through diverse means, not only through angels, but through Scriptures, circumstances and visions, answering prayers and giving signs where needed. To state that any person to whom God communicates is a prophet would mean that all Christians who have a proper relationship with God and who are in tune with His will and voice would be prophets. Of course, this is not the case, as God has chosen a select few to be teach the messages that He seeks to proclaim.

(3) Lot was Made Drunk and Lured into Incest; He did not Choose the Acts in Good Conscience

The Bible recounts that Lot was made drunk before his daughters lay with him. After the destruction of Sodom and Gomorrah, Lot and his daughters dwelt in a cave in the mountains (Gen 19:20). Lots daughters got him drunk and lay with him. The elder daughter bore a son and called his name Moab, who was the father of the Moabites (Gen 19:37), and the younger daughter bore a son and called his name Ben-Ammi, who was the father of the people of Ammon (Gen 19:38). Therefore, assigning Lot personal responsibility for his act would be no different than assigning personal responsibility to an innocent person who after being drugged loses his sense of judgment and commits some crime.

(4) Jesus as a Descendant of Lot's Incest through David's Grandmother Ruth, a Moabitess

Some critics impugn the validity of the Bible not only on the fact that it recounts the story of a man, Lot, who gets drunk and engages in incest with his daughters, but also that the product of this incest, Lot's elder daughter's son Moab, was a descendant of the Savior. Moab was an ancestor of Ruth, the Moabitess (*see* Rth 1:4), who was in turn the grandmother of David, the son of Jesse, the son of Obed (Rth 4:22), the son of Boaz (through Boaz's marriage to Ruth). David was, of course, an ancestor of Jesus (see Jesus' genealogy in Luke 3).

While Dr. Baagil does not directly make this claim, he does raise the question of Lot's incest with his daughters, and so it is opportune to treat the claim herein. First, it is necessary to concede not only that Jesus is the offspring of Lot's sin, but that he is also the offspring of equally egregious sin, including Solomon's idolatry and David's adultery and murder. It is necessary to state clearly that Jesus did not come into the world for the righteous, but for sinners (Luke 5:32). There is therefore nothing in conflict with the idea of a savior who comes into a world filled with sin that reaches even his own ancestors.

But what is remarkable in the fact that among Jesus' ancestors is a Moabite woman is not that God chose to graft the Moabite people, offspring of the sins of Lot and enemies of Israel (see Numbers 22, recounting the story of King Balak of the Moabites seeking the services of the pagan prophet Balaam to curse the Israelites), into the genealogy of Jesus, but rather, that He chose to do so by choosing a righteous woman among the Moabites who submitted to the God of Israel. Despite her mother-in-law Naomi's insisting that Ruth remain in the land of Moab after Ruth's husband had died and Naomi was to return to Bethlehem, Judah, Ruth clung to Naomi (Rth 1:14), saying to her, "Your people shall be my people, And your God, my God" (Rth 1:16).

God is therefore able to graft not only into the ancestry of Jesus as well as into His descendants righteous men and women who can be called from darkness and paganism and be called Sons of the Most High.

v.   Jacob: A Prophet who Married Two Sisters?

(1) Overview

Dr. Baagil writes that in the Christian Scriptures, "You will read of a Prophet who was married to two sisters at the same time (Genesis

29:28): 'And Jacob did so, and fulfilled her week: and he [Laban] gave him Rachel his daughter to wife also'" (p. 25).

Following is a discussion of the problems with Dr. Baagil's argument.

(a) Jacob was a Patriarch, not a Prophet

First, Jacob was not a prophet and the Bible never recorded any of his prophecies. Rather, he was a Patriarch who was the father of the twelve tribes of Israel.

(b) Jacob did not Sin Willingly; He was the Victim of Laban's Deceit

Second, Jacob's marriage to two sisters cannot be blamed on him fully; he was the victim of the deceit his uncle / father-in-law Laban. Jacob agreed to work for his uncle Laban for seven years in exchange for marriage to Laban's younger daughter Rachel (Gen 29:16-20). After seven years, Jacob demanded his wife (Gen 29:21), but Laban gave Jacob his older daughter Leah instead (Gen 29:23-34). The next morning, Jacob learned that he lay with Leah, not Rachel (Gen 29:25). Jacob protested and Laban told him to consummate Leah's bridal week and he would then give him Rachel in marriage in exchange for another seven years of work, and Jacob agreed (Gen 29:26-30). It was Jacob's love for Rachel and Laban's deceit that was the cause of Jacob's marriage to two sisters simultaneously.

(c) Jacob is not Portrayed in the Bible as Incorrigibly Sinful; He was Transformed by His God with God

Third, while it was true that Jacob was a sinful man (*e.g.*, obtaining his father Isaac's blessing through deceit by saying he was his brother Esau, dressing with Esau's clothes, saying the meat his mother prepared was game he had hunted, and wearing a goat's skin to appear hairy (Gen 27:18-29)), he was later transformed in his encounter with God (Gen 32).

vi. King David's Adultery

(1) Overview

Dr. Baagil writes, "And another Prophet accused of adultery (II Samuel 11:4-5): 'And David sent messengers, and took her [the wife of Uriah]; and she came in unto him, and he lay with her; for she was purified from her uncleanness; and she returned unto her house. And the woman conceived, and sent and told David, and said, I am with child'" (p. 25).

(2) David's Sin and Repentance

It is true that David sent for Bathsheba, lay with her (2Sa 11:4) and that she conceived (2Sa 11:5). However, after Nathan came to David confronted David over his sin, (2Sa 12:7-12), David recognized that he "sinned against the Lord" (2Sa 12:13) and repented. He paid the price for his sin: as prophesied by Nathan (2Sa 12:14), David's child born to Bathsheba died after seven days of illness (2Sa 12:15-18).

(3) King David a Prophet?

King David cannot be said to be a prophet in the full sense of the word. While it is true that he did write some messianic prophesies (*e.g.*, Psalm 41:9 ("Even My bosom friend in whom I trusted, who ate of My bread, has lifted his heel against Me") is a Messianic prophecy foreshadowing John 13:18 (He that eats bread with Me hath lifted up his heel against Me"), he was not called to the full-time prophetic office, as were, for example, Samuel, Nathan, Isaiah, Jeremiah, Ezekiel and Daniel. David's primary role was that of King.

Of course, the previously-articulated argument with respect to the sins of prophets not undermining the validity of the Scriptures holds, for "all have sinned and fall short of the glory of God" (Rom 3:23).

(4) A Bastard in the Congregation of the Lord

Dr. Baagil continues: "How could David then be accepted in the genealogy of Jesus when it started with a person who committed adultery? *Allah* forbid it! Is this not in contradiction with what is mentioned in Deuteronomy 23:2: 'A bastard shall not enter into the congregation of the Lord; even to his tenth generation shall he not enter into the congregation of the Lord'" (p. 25).

There is a two-pronged answer to Dr. Baagil's question:

- First, and as previously mentioned, God never guaranteed that Jesus' line would be comprised of sinless persons. Rather, His Scripture declares that all are guilty of sin (Rom 3:23).
- Second, Jesus was neither a bastard nor was his ancestor Solomon a bastard. Bathsheba had become David's wife (see

2Sa 11:27) *before* Solomon was born (see 2Sa 12:24). It was David's first son through Bathsheba, not Solomon, who was a bastard and he died as an infant after seven days of illness (2Sa 12:15-18).

vii. King David's Son Ammon's Rape of Ammon's Half-Sister Tamar

(1) Overview

Dr. Baagil writes, "Another allegation of incest along with rape by Ammon the son of David on his half-sister Tamar (II Samuel 13:14): "How be it he [Ammon] would not hearken unto her voice: but being stronger than she [Tamar], forced her, and lay with her'" (p. 25-26).

It is true that Amnon, the son of David through Ahinoam, loved his half-sister Tamar, the daughter of David through Maacah, and Absalom's sister (2Sa 13:1), to the point of pretending to be ill so she would come into his bedroom to attend to and feed him (2Sa 13:3-6). When Tamar brought him food, he seized her and said "Come, lie with me" (2Sa 13:11). Tamar refused to do the disgraceful thing (2Sa 13:12), but Amnon raped her (2Sa 13:14).

(2) The Sins of the Sons of a King Does Not Undermine Christian Doctrine

It is unclear what Dr. Baagil intends to prove with this story. If he is trying to demonstrate that sinful acts are recounted in the Bible, he would have been able to find far worse stories. If he was trying to prove that the Hebrew Scriptures are false because they recount man's sinfulness, one only need to look in the world to find that the evil recounted in the Bible is a reflection of reality and history. If, however, he is trying to prove that the Bible cannot be true because the children of an Israeli king—in this case, the son of King David—must be perfect and free from sin, and that the Bible, in recounting an act of rape at the hand of David's son, cannot be true, then he must do a better job at explaining on what basis he concludes that the children of Israel's kings cannot be subject to sin. Such a principle is not a premise of orthodox Christianity by any means.

viii.   King David's Son Absalom's Rape of David's Concubines

(1) Overview

Dr. Baagil writes, "Still another multiple rape, by Absalom on David's concubines, was told in II Samuel 16:33: 'So they spread Absalom a tent upon the top of the house, and Absalom went in unto his father's concubines in the sight of all Israel.'" (p. 26).

(2) Dr. Baagil's Inaccuracies

Dr. Baagil's reference and recounting are both incorrect. First, the Reference should be II Samuel 16:22, not 16:33). Second, nothing in the story indicates a "rape" or "multiple rape." The Scripture simply states that Absalom simply "slept' with the concubines: "So they pitched a tent for Absalom on the roof, and Absalom slept with his father's concubines in the sight of all Israel (2Sa 16:22)." Nothing connotes or denotes that the act was forced on the concubines.

(3) The Sins of the Sons of a King Does Not Undermine Christian Doctrine

Of course, whether by force or by will, Absalom's act was a perversion that involved both the sin of fornication and rebellion against God and the King. Dr. Baagil impugns the validity of the Hebrew Scriptures by this act, yet he does not explain how the story invalidates the Scriptures. He seems to be working on the premise that the sons of the kings of Israel must all be perfect, sinless, holy men of God, and that because the sons raped their half-sisters, slept with concubines, etc., the Scriptures cannot be true. However, he never elucidates on what basis his doctrine is based; it is certainly not a teaching of Judaism or Christianity that the sons of kings are to be sinless. In contrast, the Bible makes clear the evils that would come of a king. When the elders of Israel asked to be ruled by a king (1Sa 8:4-5), God told Samuel to warn the people of Israel of the behavior of the king who would rule over them (1Sa 8:9).

So Samuel told the people of Israel that the king who would rule over them would take their sons and appoint them to his chariots and armed forces, put them to work in his fields and to make weapons of war; he would make their daughters perfumers and cooks; he would take their fields and vineyards and a tenth of their grain and take their servants to put to work for him (1Sa 8:10-16); even the people would become his slaves (1Sa 8:17). The prophet Samuel predicted that the people would cry out to God because of the behavior of the king (1Sa 8:18).

Therefore, the Scripture is clear that, far from being perfect and sinless, the king would be a cause of distress over Israel. If such is true of the king, the anointed of God, then what could be expected of his sons? Indeed, the wickedness of David's sons Amnon and Absalom is not in contradiction with any of the Bible's teachings on the total depravity of man; in fact, it can even be said to have been anticipated by the prophet Samuel's warning to Israel.

ix. Judah's Incest with His Daughter-in-Law Tamar

(1) Overview

Dr. Baagil writes, "Another incest, by Judah and Tamar his daughter-in-law: Judah on his way to Timnath to shear his sheep saw Tamar; he thought her to be a harlot because she had her face covered (Genesis 38:18): '... And he [Judah] gave his [signet, bracelet and staff] her [*sic.*], and came in unto her and she conceived by him'" (p. 26).

(2) The Proper Context: Judah's Acts was not One of Incest

For the proper context, the following is the full story of Judah and his daughter-in-law Tamar: Judah's first son Er married Tamar (Gen 38:6), but because Er did evil, God put him to death (Gen 38:7). Judah then had his second son Onan sleep with Tamar to create offspring for Er (Gen 38:8), but Onan, seeing that the offspring would not be his, let his seed spill on the earth (Gen 38:9). Because of this act, God put him to death (Gen 38:10). Then Judah sent Tamar back to her father's house until his third son Shelah came of age (Gen 38:11).

Judah's wife Bathshua died and Judah went to Timnah (Gen 38:12). When Tamar heard this, she took off her widow's clothing, covered herself with a veil and went to Timnah, knowing that Shelah was now a man, but she had not been made his wife as promised (Gen 38:13-14). When Judah saw her, he mistook Tamar for a harlot (Gen 38:15) and asked to sleep with her (Gen 38:16) in exchange for a young goat (Gen 38:17). He did and she became pregnant by him (Gen 38:18).

When the affair came to light, Judah recognized that Tamar was more righteous than he, because he would not give her to his son Shelah as promised (Gen 38:26). Tamar gave birth to twin boys: Perez and Zerah (Gen 38:27-30).

Because Tamar was not Judah's blood relative, the two were not guilty of incest. However, Judah was guilty of breaching his promise and duty to give Tamar his son Shelah as Ur and Onan's kinsman-redeemer, of desiring to sleep with a harlot and of committing fornication.

(3) Judah was not a Prophet

By including the story of Judah with that of other biblical characters such as Noah, Solomon and David, who Dr. Baagil believes are prophets, Dr. Baagil seems to imply that Judah was a prophet and therefore not subject to sin. However, nothing in the Bible or even the *Qur'an* supports the claim that Judah was a prophet. There is no record of any of his prophecies in the Hebrew and Christian traditions, and the *Qur'an* makes no mention of Judah or of his being a prophet. Like the rest of mankind, he was a man born into a fallen world and subject to sin.

c. Conclusion

Dr. Baagil concludes, "Although Jews and Muslims are archenemies, no Muslim would dare to write a book and stamp any Israelite Prophet like Judah, David, Jesus, etc. (*Allah*'s blessings and peace be upon all of them forever and ever) with rape, adultery, incest or prostitution. All Prophets were sent by *Allah* for the guidance of mankind. Do you think that God had sent the wrong people for guidance? (p. 26)."

Dr. Baagil's statement is problematic for two reasons. First, it includes Jesus in a list of individuals who are allegedly accused by Christians of rape, adultery, incest or prostitution. Nowhere in the Scriptures or in any of the writings of the orthodox Church fathers is Jesus accused of any such sins.

Second, Dr. Baagil picks other figures that are accused in the Hebrew Scriptures of engaging in sinful acts, labels them prophets, and then charges the Scriptures of corruption by arguing that because God cannot use sinful men to speak to His people, the Scriptures must be corrupt by attributing sinful behavior to prophets. Yet Dr. Baagil never offers any evidence to support his argument that the figures as diverse as Lot and Aaron that he picks were prophets. Presumably, he picks these individuals on the basis that they are mentioned in the *Qur'an* as prophets (*see, e.g.,* 4:163: "Surely We have revealed to thee as We revealed to Noah and the prophets after him, and We revealed to Abraham and Ishmael and Isaac and Jacob and the tribes, and Jesus and Job and Jonah and Aaron and Solomon, and We gave to David a scripture").

However, such an approach is problematic for several reasons. First, Dr. Baagil employs a circular argument. He attacks the validity of the Hebrew Scriptures by approaching them through the standard of Islam's Scriptures. This approach can only work if Islam's Scriptures are true, but this very question is a subject of dispute in the book. In other words, Dr. Baagil operates on the assumption that the Hebrew Scriptures are false because they contradict Islam's Scriptures before he has even proven that the latter are truly God's word.

There are several other problems with Dr. Baagil's argument. These will be discussed at length below, but suffice it to say for now that Dr. Baagil's arguments are deeply flawed given the incredibility of the claim that God had sent these dozens of prophets throughout the millennia, yet all of their prophecies have been lost or corrupted except that of Muhammad. It is incredible that God would allow all but one prophet's prophecy to be preserved, and then that one prophet's prophecy would contradict the uniform record that the other dozens of "corrupt" prophecies have preserved in harmony.

Another problem is the incredibility of the claim that God would raise these dozens of these so called "prophets" of Islam, from Jacob, to Lot, to Moses, to Aaron, to David, to Solomon, to Job, Jonah and Jesus, all from the seed of Isaac, and then at once, without once, without any clear reason or explanation, he would cease Isaac's prophetic line, from which all of these prophets came, and then draw out one, final prophet from the line of Ishmael.

3.   Jesus as the Son of God

a.   *Claim I: Jesus was the Son of God in a Figurative, Affectionate Sense, Like the Many Other Sons of God Referenced in the Scriptures*

i.   Dr. Baagil's General Argument

(1) Overview

Dr. Baagil writes, "you will see in many passages in the Bible 'Son of God' which signifies love and affection, nearness to God, not applied to Jesus alone. You will see sons and daughters of God (II

Corinthians 6:18): 'And will be a Father unto you, and ye shall be my sons and daughters, saith the Lord Almighty.' In view of these and other passages in the Bible, there is no reason whatsoever why Jesus should be regarded as Son of God in a literal or unique sense" (p. 42).

(2) Answer: There Are Many Sons of God, But Only One Begotten Son

While the Bible repeatedly refers to sons and daughters of God, or of God being a "father," it refers only to Jesus as God's "begotten son."

(a) Many Sons of God

It is true that many in the Bible are referred to as "sons," "daughters" or "children" of God. There are many explanations for this:

-   Genesis refers to "sons of God" twice: Men increased on the earth (Gen 6:1) and the *sons of God* saw that the daughters of men were pleasing and took them as wives (Gen 6:2). God limited man's days to 120 years (Gen 6:3). There were men of great strength in those days. When the *sons of God* had connection with the daughters of men, they gave birth to men of great name (Gen 6:4). Some interpret these references to "sons of God" as referring to angels; others interpret them to mean "godly men" (as opposed to sinful women).
-   Job refers repeatedly to "sons of God": When the *sons of God* came to present themselves before Jehovah, Satan also came among them (Job 1:6). The Lord asked Satan whether he considered Job, a perfect and an upright man (Job 1:8); The *sons of God* again came to present themselves before the Lord, and Satan came also before the Lord (Job 2:1). The Lord asked Satan whether he had considered Job, a perfect and an upright man, who maintains his integrity despite temptation (Job 2:3). Some editions translate "*sons of God*" as "angels"; the NIV cites Psa 148:2-3, which states, "praise God, all his angels, praise Him, all his host, praise Him, sun and moon; praise him, all you stars of light." Job 38:7 states that stars sang together and angels "*sons of God*" shouted for joy. Psa 148:2-3 commands the angels and the stars to praise Him.

- "Sons of God" is frequently used to mean "ruler" or "judge." In Psalms, "sons of God" are translated as "sons of the Mighty" (ASV), "sons of the gods" (BBE), "heavenly beings" (ESV, ISV, RSV) or "mighty ones" (NKJV). According to the NIV study Bible note at Psa 82:1, "In the language of the OT—and in accordance with the conceptual world of the ancient Near East—rulers and judges, as deputies of the heavenly King, could be given the honorific title 'god'" or be called "son of God." The fact that these "gods" or "sons of god" were mere men is attested to by the fact that they "will come to death like men, falling like one of the rulers of the earth" (Psa 82:7).
- The Israelites are referred to as "children of God" in a figurative sense denoting affection and proximity to God: You are the *children* of the Lord your God; you shall not cut yourselves nor shave the front of your head for the dead (Deu 14:1). I will say to the north, 'Give them up!' And to the south, 'Do not keep them back!' Bring My *sons* from afar and My *daughters* from the ends of the earth (Isa 43:6).
- Those with faith in Jesus and the righteous generally are referred to as "children of God": Being high priest that year, [Caiaphas] prophesied that Jesus would die for the nation (John 11:51) and not for that nation only, but also that He would gather together in one the *children of God* who were scattered abroad (John 11:52). Peacemakers are called "sons of God," at least in a figurative sense (Mat 5:9). Those that are worthy to attain to the resurrection from the dead and the next life are equal to the angels and are "sons of God" (Luke 20:36). The creation also will be delivered from the bondage of corruption into the liberty of the glory of the *children of God* (Rom 8:21).

What these passages mean is that "son of God" is not used in any translation of the Bible as referring exclusively to Jesus. Rather, "son of God" can be used in many senses, to refer to "godly men," "angels," "rulers," "judges," the "Israelites" or "believers in Jesus."

(b) Yet There Is Only One "Begotten" Son of God

Although there are many "sons," "daughters" and "children" of God, Jesus is referred to specifically as the "Only Begotten Son of God":

- No one has seen God at any time. The *only begotten Son*, who is at the bosom of the Father, has declared Him (John 1:18).
- For God had such love for the world that he gave his *only begotten Son*, so that whoever has faith in him may not come to destruction but have eternal life (John 3:16).
- The love of God was made clear to us when he sent *his only begotten Son* into the world so that we might have life through him (1Jo 4:9).

ii. David Was God's "Begotten Son"; Therefore, Jesus Was Not God's Only Begotten son

(1) Overview

Dr. Baagil writes (p. 41):

> Long before Jesus was born, God said to David (Psalm 2.7): "I will declare the decree: the Lord hath said unto me [David], Thou art my Son; this day have I begotten thee." So David is also God's begotten Son. The meaning of Son of God is not literal but metaphorical. It can be any one who is beloved by God. Jesus also said that God is not only his Father but also your Father (Matthew 5:45, 48).

It is necessary to point out that Dr. Baagil is correct in stating that Psalm 2 may be a reference to David. However, it may also be interpreted as a reference to Jesus, because of its reference to the "Anointed One" (Psa 2:2) and "King of Zion" (Psa 2:6). It is true that David was anointed and King of Zion (Jerusalem), but so too was Jesus. "Anointed One" and "Son" in Psalm 2 have been interpreted to refer to Jesus (*see, e.g.*, the *NIV Study Bible* notes at Psa 2:2: "The psalm refers to the Davidic king and is ultimately fulfilled in Christ. The English word 'Messiah' comes from the Hebrew word for 'anointed one,' and the English word 'Christ' from the Greek word for 'anointed one'"). "Anointed One" and "Son" may, however, also be references to King David or any of David's heirs.

Dr. Baagil continues (p. 42):

> So you will see in many passages in the Bible "Son of God" which signifies love and affection, nearness to God, not applied to Jesus alone. You will see sons and daughters of God (II Corinthians 6:18): "And will be a Father unto you, and ye shall be my sons and daughters, saith the Lord Almighty." In view of these and other

passages in the Bible, there is no reason whatsoever why Jesus should be regarded as Son of God in a literal or unique sense.

Why do you consider Adam then not as Son of God. He lacked both father and mother, and is also called Son of God in Luke 3:38: "... Seth, which was the son of Adam, which was the son of God." Read Hebrews 7:3.

Who is he? The answer is in Hebrews 7:1: "Melchisedec, king of Salem, priest of the most high God, who met Abraham. . ." He is more unique than Jesus or Adam. Why is he not preferred to be son of God or God himself?

(2) Answer: "Begotten" Is Not an Accurate Translation of Psalm 2:7 and In Any Case, It Refers to Jesus

(a) Translations of Psalm 2:7 Vary

The translations of the Psalms vary in how they render "son" in Psalm 2:7. The ASV, Darby, ESV, KJV, NKJV and RSV refer specifically to a "begotten" son. However, other translations render the phrase differently: the BBE states, "this day have I given you being" and the ISV and NIV state, "today I have become your father" (Psa 2:7).

(b) In Any Case, Psalm 2:7 Refers to Jesus

However the phrase is translated, it appears directed at Jesus. It is important to remember that the Psalms are prophetic in nature and therefore often refer to things to come. In line with this, they are frequently referring to Jesus as the Messiah and Son of God. Consider, for example, the Messianic Prophecy of Psalm 41:9, which declares, "Even My bosom friend in whom I trusted, who ate of My bread, has lifted his heel against Me" (foreshadowing John 13:18: "that the Scripture may be fulfilled, He that eats bread with Me has lifted up his heel against Me") and Psalm 69:9, which declares "zeal for Thy house has consumed Me, and the insults of those who insult Thee have fallen on Me" (foreshadowing John 2:15-17: "when He had made a scourge of small cords, He drove them all out of the Temple, and the sheep, and the oxen; and poured out the changers' money, and overthrew the tables; And said unto them that sold doves, Take these things hence; make not My Father's House an house of merchandise. And His disciples remembered that it was written, Zeal of your house has consumed me"). Therefore, if David in Psalm 2:7 did in fact refer to God's begotten son, then the same would be referring to Jesus, who was in David's line and God's only begotten Son (John 1:18; John 3:16; 1Jo 4:9).

That Psalm 2:7 refers to Jesus is made clear by Luke the Evangelist, who in the Book of Acts 13:33, quotes Psalm 2:7, where he contrasts David, who was buried with his fathers and whose body was corrupted, with Jesus, whose body never decayed (Acts 13:35, quoting Psa 16:10). Luke considers Jesus to be the fulfillment of Psalm 2:7.

That Psalm 2:7 refers to Jesus is further made clear by the author of Hebrews, who describes Jesus as the reflection of God's glory and the exact likeness of his being, holding everything together by His word, who cleansed our sins, sat down at the right hand of the Father (Heb 1:3) and became superior to the angels (Heb 1:4). The author then goes on to quote Psalm 2:7, saying that God never said to any angel, You are my Son. Today I have become your Father (Heb 1:5). In contrasting Jesus to the angels, the implication is thus that God called Jesus His Son.

(c) If the Phrase were Directed at David, then It Would Be Appropriate to Interpret It Figuratively

If the phrase were not directed to Jesus but to David, then it should be taken into account that in the ancient Near East, the relationship between a great king and a subject king that owed him allegiance was often express through the words "father" and "son." Thus, in light of this, David should be viewed as God's "son" in the sense of His servant, who ruled by God's authority.

iii. Conclusion

While many persons in the Bible, including Jesus, Adam, angels, Israelites in the Old Testament, Christians in the New Testament and even angels are referred to as "children," "sons" or "daughters" of God and God is referred to as their "father," Jesus alone holds the title "only begotten Son." Jesus is distinct from all of these other categories in the following way:

- Unlike Adam and the angels, Jesus was not created by God. Rather, Jesus is a member of the God who existed from the beginning (John 1:1).

- Unlike all other men and women, Jesus did not have a physical father in the flesh; rather, His father was God.

Perhaps Psalm 2:7 does indeed include a reference to "begotten Son," but even if this were the case, the various New Testament writings, including Acts 13:33 and Hebrews 1:5, make clear that this reference was intended to honor Jesus as God's only begotten Son.

b. Claim II: Jesus Was No More a Son of God than Adam Was

"Why do you consider Adam then not as Son of God. He lacked both father and mother, and is also called Son of God in Luke 3:38: "... Seth, which was the son of Adam, which was the son of God'" (p. 42).

Christians consider Adam a son of God in the sense of having been directly created by God, without earthly parents, in accordance with Luke 3:38: Jesus was … the son of Seth, the son of Adam, the son of God. However, Adam was not begotten of God in the sense that Jesus was. He did not have the same "genetic material" that Jesus had:

- Jesus, unlike Adam, had divine knowledge. He knew the details about His own death, saying He would go to Jerusalem, suffer many things at the hands of the chief priests and scribes, be killed, and then be resurrected the third day (Mat 16:21). He had knowledge about a woman's life whom He had never previously met (John 4:16-19) and about Nathaniel who was under a fig-tree (John 1:47-49). Adam, in contrast, did not even have knowledge of good and evil or that he was naked before eating the forbidden fruit (Gen 2:9; Gen 3:6-7).
- Unlike Adam, who was created at a particular point in history, Jesus was uncreated and existed since the beginning (John 1:1). Jesus is "from everlasting" (Mic 5:2), which is exactly what Psalm 93:2 and Isaiah 63:16 say about God! Also, the New Testament repeatedly refers to Jesus as God ("The Word [Jesus] was God" (John 1:1); Thomas referred to Jesus as "My Lord and my God" (John 20:28); "We are in Him who is true, in His Son Jesus Christ. This is the true God and eternal life" (1Jn 5:20)). Therefore, unlike Adam, Jesus is God and must therefore have God's qualities, including his eternal nature (Psa 93:2; Isa 63:16).

Therefore, Adam, while being a "son of God" in the sense of being God's creation, was not of the same nature of Christ, God's only "begotten" son (John 3:16; 1Jo 4:9; John 1:18).

c. Claim III: "Without Father, without Mother" of Hebrews 7:3 Points to Melchizedek, not Jesus

Dr. Baagil goes on to state that "Without father, without mother, without descent, having neither beginning of days, nor end of life; but made like unto the Son of God; abideth a priest continually" of Hebrews 7:3 refers to "Melchizedek, king of Salem, priest of the most high God, who met Abraham," and who is "more unique than Jesus" (p. 42). Why, Dr. Baagil asks, "is he not preferred to be son of God or God himself?" (p. 42).

Dr. Baagil points here to Melchizedek, arguably the most mysterious figure that appears in the whole of the Scriptures. First, it is not clear exactly who Melchizedek is. Some commentators view him as a Canaanite priest, who somehow came to know of the true God of Abraham, since he is described as priest of "the Most High God" (Gen 14:18). One may view Melchizedek as God the father, because he was "[w]ithout father, without mother, without genealogy" (Heb 7:3). An overwhelming number of similarities with Jesus point to his being not just a "Christ type," but an early manifestation of Jesus. Consider, for example:

- Melchizedek was "King of Salem," which also means "king of peace" (Heb 7:1, 2). Jesus is the "Prince of Peace" (Isa 9:6). In a sense, Jesus is also "King of Peace." Isaiah 11 states that "a new king will come" (Isa 11:1) and at that time, "wolves will live in peace with lambs" (Isa 11:6).
- When Abram returned from the rescue of Lot (Gen 14:16), Melchizedek brought out bread and wine (Gen 14:18). Jesus offered his disciples bread and wine at the last supper (Mat 26:26-28). This bread and wine was His flesh and blood unto the salvation of all who believed (Mat 26:26-28).
- Jesus said that "Abraham rejoiced to see my day; and he saw it, and was glad" (John 8:56). When did Abraham see Jesus' day? Presumably in Melchizedek, an Old Testament manifestation of Christ.
- Melchizedek was called a "priest of the Most High God" and "high priest" in the Scripture (see Gen 14:18; Heb 4:14-15;

Heb 5:5-6; Heb 5:10, etc.). But only Jesus and the Aaronic priests are selected by the true God to represent God (*see generally* Heb 7). Therefore, if Melchizedek was a priest of the "Most High God" (Gen 14:18), he must either be an Aaronic priest or Jesus. He is not an Aaronic priest because he was not a descendent of Levi (Heb 7:5-6). Melchizedek may therefore be Jesus, whose genealogy is also not derived from Levi.

- Heb 7:3 states that Melchizedek was "made like the Son of God" (Heb 7:3). This would suggest that he may be Jesus.

Regardless of whether Melchizedek was a Canaanite priest or an Old Testament manifestation of Jesus, the selection of Jesus as "son of God" is not one made arbitrarily by Christians based on which candidate is most "unique," as Dr. Baagil suggests on page 42. The early church did not gather together potential candidates to whom to assign the title "Son of God"; rather, they recognize Jesus as the Son of God because they believe His claims to be the same, as recorded in His answer to the high priest when asked if he was the Son of God (Mat 26:63) ("It is as you said" (Mat 26:64)), in his defense to the Jews of the Temple ("I have said, I am the Son of God" (John 10:36)) and elsewhere throughout the Gospels (*see* Mat 8:29; Mat 14:33; Mat 27:41-43; Mark 1:1; Mark 3:11; Mark 15:39; Luke 1:35; etc.).

d. Claim IV: Jesus Refused to be Called Son of God

Dr. Baagil writes that "Jesus called himself Son of man and refused to be called Son of God" (p. 42). He points to Luke 4:41 to support his point: "And demons also came out of many, crying out and saying, "You are the Christ, the Son of God!" And He, rebuking them, did not allow them to speak, for they knew that He was the Christ."

Dr. Baagil's statement is flawed for several reasons discussed below.

i. Christ Does Not Rebuke the Demons in order to Deny that He is the Christ

Christ does not rebuke the demons in order to deny that He was the Son of God or Christ (Messiah). As Luke points out clearly, the demons *knew* Jesus was the Christ (Luke 4:41), not that they merely suspected or believed it. Jesus rebuked the demons because He did not want His divinity known early on in his ministry, which is why He instructed the raising of Jairus' daughter from the dead not to be told (Mark 5:43) and that the disciples tell no one that He was the Christ (Mat 16:20), explaining to them that He would first need to go to Jerusalem, be put to death and then rise from the dead (Mat 16:21).

ii. Jesus Does Not "Refuse" to be Called Son of God

Dr. Baagil's statement that Jesus "refused to be called Son of God" (p. 42) is false. Consider the following:

- Jesus allowed his disciples to call him Son of God. When Peter said that Jesus is the Christ, the Son of the living God (Mat 16:16), Jesus did not refuse the title. Rather, He blessed Peter and declared that Peter received this knowledge from Jesus' "Father who is in heaven" (Mat 16:17). Similar examples can be found in Mat 8:29, Mat 14:33, Mark 3:11 and Mark 15:39.
- When Jesus was put on trial, Jesus allowed His accusers to call him Son of God. He even positively affirmed to the high priest that He was the Son of God: when the high priest asked Jesus, "Tell us if You are the Christ, the Son of God!" (Mat 26:63), Jesus answered, "It is as you said" (Mat 26:64).
- The Jews in the temple asked Jesus, "How long are you going to keep us in suspense? If you are the Christ, say so clearly" (John 10:24). Jesus answers them, saying, "That which my Father has given to me has more value than all; and no one is able to take anything out of the Father's hand. I and my Father are one" (John 10:29-30). The Jews understand His implication to be the Son of God, and Jesus affirms this implication when he says, "do you say of Him whom the Father sanctified and sent into the world, 'You are blaspheming,' because I said, 'I am the Son of God'?" (John 10:36).

iii. Why Jesus Rebuked the Demons for Calling Him Son of God

So why did Jesus then rebuke the demons for calling him the Son of God, if Jesus allowed his disciples and his accusers to call Him the Son of God? There are two possible explanations:

(1) The Timing of the Revelation

The timing for revealing Jesus' true identity had not yet come. This is why Jesus allowed his inner circle of disciples to call him the Son of

God, but forbade them from disclosing this knowledge to others. For example, when Peter disclosed his knowledge that Jesus was the Christ and Son of God (Mat 16:16), Jesus blessed him (Mat 16:17-19), but ordered that His disciples give no man word that he was the Christ (Mat 16:20). However, later on, when Jesus' was accused by the high priests and scribes, he openly admitted that He was the Son of God (Mat 26:64), because the timing of the revelation of his identity was near. Before His arrest and accusation, Jesus avoided openly revealing His divinity. For example, when the chief priests and the scribes and the rulers came to him and asked by what authority was He teaching (Luke 20:2), rather than reveal His authority, Jesus avoided the question by answering them with another question (Luke 20:3): Was the baptism of John from heaven or of men (Luke 20:4)?

The fact that Jesus did not reveal his identity clearly in public before his arrest and trial is made clear by his Jewish accusers in the temple, who confront Him, asking: "How long are you going to keep us in suspense? If you are the Christ, say so clearly" (John 10:24). Jesus does not unequivocally reveal that He is Christ and Son of God, but He implies it strong enough to cause them to accuse Him of blasphemy (John 10:33). Jesus answered them, saying: "That which my Father has given to me has more value than all; and no one is able to take anything out of the Father's hand. I and my Father are one" (John 10:29-30).

The problem, however, with the theory that Jesus avoided revealing that He was the Son of God until the proper timing (after His arrest and trial) is that He clearly reveals His identity to His Jewish confronters at the temple after they picked up stones to stone him. He said: "Is there not a saying in your law, I said, You are gods? If he said they were gods, to whom the word of God came and the writings may not be broken, do you say of him whom the Father made holy and sent into the world, Your words are evil; because I said, I am God's Son?" (John 10:34-36).

Yet perhaps this account is given to us to demonstrate what *would* have happened had Jesus openly declared His divine identity. Here, the Jews picked up stones to stone Jesus (John 10:31) and tried to seize Him, but He escaped their grasp (John 10:39). Had He continued to declare He was the Son of God, there certainly would have been multiple attempts to kill him, perhaps even riots against Him, attempting to kill Him before the Roman authorities arrested Him and put him to death on the cross, in fulfillment of the Old Testament prophecies that came to pass in the crucifixion (*e.g.*, that wounds would be made in his hands and feet and his clothes would be divided by chance (Psa 22:16-18); that He would be numbered with the evil-doers and pray for them (Isa 53:12); that His side would be pierced (Zec 12:10); His bones would not be broken (Psa 34:20); etc.). John even remarks that the decision of the soldiers to pierce Jesus' side rather than break His legs "came about so that the Scriptures might be fulfilled" (John 19:36).

Therefore, it is possible that the incidents in John 10, where Jesus reveals His divine nature, is offered to give the reader a glimpse as to why Jesus reserved revealing his divine nature until the appointed time.

(2) Jesus Did Not Wish for Demons to Serve As His Witnesses

A second explanation as to why Jesus silenced the demons is that He did not wish to be associated with demonic powers. Jesus is repeatedly accused of having a demon or of being demon-possessed:

- The scribes who came down from Jerusalem said, He has Beelzebub, and by the ruler of evil spirits, he sends evil spirits out of men (Mark 3:22).
- The Jews said to Jesus, Are we not right in saying that you are of Samaria and have a demon? Jesus answered, I do not have a demon; but I give honor to my Father and you do not give honor to me (John 8:48-49).
- Many of the Jews were saying, He has a demon and is out of his mind; why do you give ear to him? (John 10:20).

These Jews sought to undermine Jesus' authority by attributing his miracles and powers to the devil.

In order to completely separate himself from the realm of darkness, Jesus sought to silence the demons that pronounced that He was the Son of God. He would not allow Satan to gain a foothold in the lives of people by allowing Satan's minions to proclaim truths about Jesus. In other words, He would not allow Himself to be associated with evil.

For this same reason, Paul was greatly troubled by the slave girl who practiced divination and declared over a number of days that Paul and the disciples were "servants of the Most High God, who are giving news of the way of salvation" (Acts 16:17). Paul said to the spirit, "I give you orders in the name of Jesus Christ, to come out of her" (Acts

16:18), probably because he did not want to be associated with divination, given the Old Testament's strong condemnation of witchcraft.

(3) Conclusion

Ultimately, we do not know why Jesus rebuked the demons for calling Him the Son of God. The two explanations presented above are possible, but the Scriptures do not give us the exact reasons. However, what we do know is that Dr. Baagil's conclusion from Jesus' rebuking the demons is wrong. If Jesus rebuked the demons for calling Him the Son of God because He was not the Son of God, then why would He accept the title from Peter (Mat 16:16-17), the Jews in the temple (John 10:29-36) and the high priest (Mat 26:63-64).

Moreover, considering Jesus' rebuking the demons for calling Him the Son of God as evidence that He was not the Son of God would be like considering Paul's rebuking the demon in the slave girl who declared that Paul was a servant of God giving news of the way of salvation (Acts 16:17) as evidence that Paul was not a servant of God giving news of the way of salvation. Of course, Paul *did* believe himself to be a servant of God giving news of salvation, and yet rebuked and drove the demon out of the girl (Acts 16:18).

4. The Divinity of Jesus, Divine Sonship of Jesus and Atonement as "Doctrines of Men"

a. *Manmade Doctrine*

The author writes that Jesus, in stating "in vain they do worship me, teaching for doctrines the commandments of men," was referring to the false, manmade doctrines of the divinity of Jesus, divine Sonship of Jesus and atonement (p. 19). However, this is problematic for the following reasons:

- The context of Jesus' statement does not support Dr. Baagil's conclusion. Jesus' statement, which comes from Matthew 15:9, is referring to the transgression of Jesus' disciples of the traditions of the elders with respect to the washing of hands ("Why do Your disciples transgress the tradition of the elders? For they do not wash their hands when they eat bread"). Jesus criticized the scribes and Pharisees by stating that they teach as the doctrines the commandments of men. Nowhere do discussions of Jesus' divinity or sonship or of the atonement come up during the conversation.

- Jesus himself taught his divinity and sonship and the doctrine of the atonement elsewhere in the Scriptures. Dr. Baagil's reading is further flawed because Jesus taught his divinity and sonship and the doctrine of the atonement throughout the Scriptures. For example, when the high priest asked Jesus, "Tell us if You are the Christ, the Son of God!" (Mat 26:63), Jesus answered, "It is as you said" (Mat 26:64). Moreover, Jesus invoked the divine name upon himself: "Jesus said to them, "Most assuredly, I say to you, before Abraham was, I AM" (John 8:58). He affirms the doctrine of the atonement in John, stating that He died so others may have life: "I am the good shepherd. The good shepherd gives His life for the sheep … As the Father knows Me, even so I know the Father; and I lay down My life for the sheep" (John 10:11, 15). He also states, "This is my blood of the covenant, which is poured out for many for the forgiveness of sins" (Mat 26:28).
- John the Baptist also affirmed the atonement in exclaiming upon seeing Christ, "Behold! The Lamb of God who takes away the sin of the world!" (John 1:29).

Dr. Baagil continues to repeat these arguments throughout the book, misinterpreting the meaning of several verses of Scriptures and of the doctrine of the Trinity. He writes:

> All doctrines of modern Christianity are made by men: the Trinity, Divine Sonship of Jesus, Divinity of Jesus Christ, Original Sin and Atonement. From Jesus' own sayings, recorded in the New Testament, it is clear that he never claimed divinity or identity to God: "I do nothing of myself" (John 8:28); "My Father is greater than I" (john 14:28); "The Lord our God is one Lord" (Mark 12:29); "My God, my God, why hast thou forsaken me?" (Mark 15:34); "Father, into thy hands I commend my spirit" (Luke 23:46).

We treat his concerns one-by-one below:

- Dr. Baagil argues that Jesus never claimed divinity or identity to God, and he cites the following verses: John 8:28 ("I do nothing of myself"); John 14:28 ("My Father is greater than I"); Mark 12:29 ("The Lord our God is one Lord"); and Mark 15:34 ("My God, my God, why hast thou forsaken me?"). All of these verses demonstrate Dr. Baagil's continued misunderstanding of the Trinity. It is true, as Jesus states, that the Lord our God is "one Lord." However, He is one Lord in three persons. One of these is the Son; the others are the Father and Holy Spirit. The three are distinct but one. Jesus is able to state that God is one and yet declare himself to be part of God because he is one of the persons of the Trinity. There is no contradiction with a proper understanding of the Trinity.

- Dr. Baagil cites Luke 23:46: "Father, into thy hands I commend my spirit." It is bewildering that Dr. Baagil cites this verse to support his argument against the Divine Sonship of Jesus because in this very verse, Jesus clearly and explicitly refers to God as "Father." It would be harder to find clearer evidence than this of Jesus' Sonship.

b. Jesus Could Do No Miracles on His Own or Without Man's Faith

i. Overview

Dr. Baagil further writes that "Jesus also did the miracles with the grace of God, as he himself said (John 5:30): 'I can of mine own self do nothing ...' and (Luke 11:20): 'But if I with the finger of God cast out devils, no doubt the Kingdom of God is come upon you.'

"All miracles performed by Jesus had been done by previous prophets, disciples, and even unbelievers. On the other hand, Jesus could do no mighty work where there was unbelief (Mark 6:5,6): "And he could there do no mighty work, save that he laid his hands upon a few sick folk, and healed them. And he marveled because of their unbelief. And he went around about the villages, teaching'" (p. 38).

Dr. Baagil's central argument is therefore that Jesus was a prophet, not God, because unlike God, Jesus was limited in what He could do. Dr. Baagil argues two separate points, each of which we respond to in turn: (i) without God, Jesus can do nothing; and (ii) Jesus cannot perform miracles without men's faith.

ii. Without God, Jesus can do Nothing

Jesus says "I can of mine own self [i.e., without God] do nothing" (John 5:30). This verse does not undermine Jesus' divinity, but rather reinforces the doctrine of the Trinity. Jesus is God and is part of the Trinity. He is integral to the Godhead. His oneness with God is the source of Jesus' divinity. Therefore, without God, Jesus could do nothing.

iii. Without Men's faith, Jesus Could not Perform Mighty Works

(1) Overview

In his country (Mark 6:1) (Nazareth), Jesus "could do no might work, save that he laid his hands upon a few sick folk, and healed them. And he marveled because of their unbelief" (Mark 6:5-6). Dr. Baagil concludes that "Jesus could do no mighty work where there was unbelief" (p. 38), implying that Jesus could not be God because there are no limitations on God or on His mighty works.

Of course, such a teaching would be inconsistent with the Bible. Jesus, who was God, created the universe in seven days. No man's faith was present when God performed this mighty work. Therefore, we should take a different approach to Mark 6:5 and come to understand its meaning based on context.

Mark 6:5 clearly indicates the nature of the "mighty works" being referenced. It states that Jesus "could do no mighty work there, *except that He laid His hands on a few sick people and healed them.*" The second clause of the sentence begins with *except*. Therefore, what follows *except*—laying hands on a few sick people and healing them— are kinds of "mighty works" that Jesus was able to perform. The "mighty works" are therefore those through which Christ ministered: healing, blessing, feeding, freeing from demons and so forth.

It is important to note that these works, almost without exception required men and women to come forth to Jesus in faith and petition. Consider, for example:

- The centurion who came to Jesus and told Him that His servant was home sick and tormented (Mat 8:5-6). The centurion requested that Jesus say the word to heal the servant (Mat 8:8). Jesus marveled at his faith (Mat 8:10) and granted the petition, healing the servant (Mat 8:13).
- The ruler of the synagogue Jairus who fell at Jesus' feet and beseeched him to heal his daughter who was at the point of death (Mark 5:22-23). Jesus went to Jairus' home and raised the daughter from the dead (Mark 5:42).
- The woman with an issue of blood over twelve years (Mark 5:25) who came behind Jesus and touched his garment (Mark

5:27), believing it would heal her (Mark 5:28). Straightaway she felt in her body that she was healed (Mark 5:29).

- The leper who came to Jesus and worshipped him, saying, "Lord, if you are willing, you can make me clean" (Mat 8:2). The man's worship indicated his faith that Jesus was God. Jesus touched him and said "I will; be made clean." The man was straightaway cleansed (Mat 8:3).

In all of these examples, a man or woman comes to Jesus in faith and petition, asking for healing, throwing himself at Jesus' feet, worshipping him or undertaking some other act of faith, such as touching his garment. In one case, a Canaanite woman so persisted in asking Jesus to have mercy on her daughter that she likened herself to a dog that eats of the crumbs which fall from the table of their masters (Mat 15:27). At this, Jesus marveled at her faith and her daughter was healed from that hour (Mat 15:28).

(2) Exceptions

There are some exceptions where a petition is not clearly made prior to a healing or release. For example, it appears that Jesus said to the unclean spirit Legion to come out of the man before the man requested the same (Mark 5:7-8). However, the recounting is not entirely clear as to whether the man solicited being freed, but even if he did not, the reality is that the man was possessed by a demon and not in his right mind to petition that which was good or fitting for him. In any case, that the man was thankful after being set free is implied by Mark 5:19, for as Jesus was entering into the boat, the man besought Jesus that he might remain with Him.

(3) Conclusion

It is therefore clear that where men have no faith, they do not petition, and where they do not petition, God does not respond. It is not therefore that Jesus could do no great works in Nazareth because unbelief tied the hands of God. Rather, it is that God, in His humility, does not bestow His grace on those that reject it. God gave man free will. He provided prophets and signs and wonders, and even offered up the life of His Son so that man could have healing, faith and life eternal. However, God cannot force anyone to believe or to accept the graces that have been freely offered. Therefore, where people do not make application for graces, Jesus cannot grant them because doing so would be against His character. Men forfeit salvation and healing and it is against God's nature to force men to be saved, for he created man with free will, not robots. The Nazarenes unbelief and contempt of Christ, not God's will, stopped the current of mighty works in Nazareth.

This is reinforced in James: "let him ask in faith, with no doubting, he who doubts is like a wave of the sea driven and tossed by the wind. For let not that man suppose that he will receive anything from the Lord" (Jam 1:6-7). He who doubts does not receive from God, for doubt and unbelief bar closed the door to God's grace.

c. Paul as the "First" to Call Jesus the Son of God

The author goes on to state that Paul "was also the first to declare Jesus as the Son of God (Acts 9:20): 'And straightway he [Paul] preached Christ in the synagogues, that he is the Son of God'" and that therefore, "Christianity is not a teaching of Jesus but Paul" (p. 48). This statement is problematic for the following reasons:

i. Jesus Affirmed Being the Son of God before Paul became a Christian

(1) To the High Priest

On trial, when the High Priest commanded Jesus to "Tell us if You are the Christ, the Son of God" (Mat 26:63), He replied "It is as you said" (Mat 26:64). This is further made clear in Matthew 27:43, where His accusers affirm that Jesus said "I am the Son of God."

(2) To the Man Born Blind

After Jesus gave sight to the man who was blind by birth, He asked him "Do you believe in the Son of God?" (John 9:35). The man who received his sight answered and said, "Who is He, Lord, that I may believe in Him?" (John 9:36). Jesus replied, "You have both seen Him and it is He who is talking with you" (John 9:37). The blind man proclaimed "Lord, I believe!" and worshiped Jesus (John 9:38).

(3) To the Jews

Jesus further admits to the Jews that He said, "I am the Son of God" (John 10:36).

(4) To Peter

When Jesus asked the disciples "who do you say that I am?" (Mat 16:15), Peter answered and said, "You are the Christ, the Son of the living God" (Mat 16:16). Jesus did not deny this, but instead replied, "Blessed are you, Simon Bar-Jonah, for flesh and blood has not revealed this to you, but My Father who is in heaven" (Mat 16:17).

ii. Paul was not the First to Declare Jesus to be the Son of God

Multiple passages indicate that many others before Paul declared Jesus to be the Son of God. Mark opens his Gospel with "The beginning of the gospel of Jesus Christ, the Son of God." This was written before Paul became a Christian or proclaimed his gospel. Satan implied Jesus was the Son of God when he tempted Jesus by stating "If You are the Son of God, command that these stones become bread" (Mat 4:3). The demon Legion acknowledged it when he stated "What have I to do with You, Jesus, Son of the Most High God? I implore You by God that You do not torment me" (Mark 5:7). The disciples who were in the boat with Jesus, upon witnessing the wind and storm obey Him, worshiped Jesus and proclaimed "Truly You are the Son of God" (Mat 14:33). Martha also declared to Jesus, "Lord, I believe that You are the Christ, the Son of God" (John 11:27).

iii. Nathaniel Rightly Believed Jesus to be the Son of God

When the disciple Nathanael proclaimed to Jesus, "You are the Son of God!" (John 1:49), Jesus' reply was "Because I said to you, 'I saw you under the fig tree,' do you believe?" (John 1:50). Jesus here uses the word "believe." Believe in what? The implication is believe in the truth. If Jesus were only a prophet whose mission was to lead men to the one, true God, it would seem logical that He would have rebuked Nathaniel for believing and proclaiming a lie. Rather, Jesus states, "You will see greater things than these" (John 1:50), ostensibly in support of Nathaniel's belief in Jesus as the Son of God.

iv. The Unclean Spirits Knew Jesus was the Son of God

Mark proclaims that "the unclean spirits, whenever they saw Him, fell down before Him and cried out, saying, 'You are the Son of God'" (Mark 3:11). Jesus, recognizing that they knew who He was, "sternly warned them that they should not make Him known" (Mark 3:12). If

Jesus was not the Son of God, then the spirits would have been unable to make Him known, because in believing Him to be the Son of God, they would have known who He was. Jesus' warning to the spirits affirms that in proclaiming Him to be the Son of God, the spirits knew who He was.

v. Jesus never Denied that He was the Son of God

Jesus was called the Son of God by the disciples, by Martha, by the unclean spirits, by the High Priest, by Nathaniel, and by others. He never refused the title. Had Jesus been only a prophet and not the Son of God, He never would have adamantly objected to the title "Son of God" and to accepting worship. As a prophet, He would have been aware of God's prohibition on having "other Gods before Me" (Exo 20:3) and misusing God's name ("You shall not take the name of the LORD your God in vain" (Exo 20:7)). Moreover, to falsely claim to be the Son of God would be blasphemous, as understood by the Jews (see Mat 26:65), and punishable by death (Lev 24:16). A prophet of God never would have tolerated such behavior.

vi. Jesus' Raising of Lazurus from the Dead was to Glorify the "Son of God"

When Jesus heard that Lazarus was dead, He said, "This sickness is not unto death, but for the glory of God, that the Son of God may be glorified through it" (John 11:4). Who was this "Son of God" who would be glorified through Lazarus's death? It was Jesus, who went to the tomb and cried with a loud voice, "Lazarus, come forth!" (John 11:43), raising Lazarus from the dead (John 11:44). Jesus makes this clear to Martha when He reminds her, "Did I not say to you that if you would believe you would see the glory of God?" (John 11:40).

vii. God Sent His Son, Jesus, for the Salvation of the World

Jesus affirms that "God so loved the world that He gave His only begotten Son, that whoever believes in Him should not perish but have everlasting life. For God did not send His Son into the world to condemn the world, but that the world through Him might be saved" (John 3:16-17). Clearly, then, Jesus believes that God has a Son. Who is the Son who was sent to save the world? John the Baptist proclaims clearly, as he saw Jesus coming toward him, "Behold! The Lamb of God who takes away the sin of the world!" (John 1:29).

d. If Jesus Is Divine Because He was Raised up to Heaven, Then So Too Are other Prophets who were Raised up to Heaven

Dr. Baagil writes, "If you still believe that Jesus is divine because he was raised up to heaven, why don't you accept other Prophets as divine who were also raised up to heaven?" (p. 48). Dr. Baagil cites two prophets who were raised up to heaven (p. 48):

-   Elijah, who in 2 Kings, "went up by a whirlwind into heaven. And Elisha saw it" (2Ki 2:11-12).
-   Enoch, who in Genesis, "walked with God; and he was no more, for God took him" (Gen 5:24). This is repeated in Hebrews 11:5: "Heb 11:5 By faith Enoch was taken away so that he did not see death, 'and was not found, because God had taken him'; for before he was taken he had this testimony, that he pleased God." (Heb 11:5).

There are several points to remember when answering Dr. Baagil's question:

-   First, unlike Elijah and Enoch, Jesus *did* die. It is precisely the death of the Messiah that is central to the Christian teaching of the atonement and the sacrifice that opened the way to salvation: "For God so loved the world that He gave His only begotten Son, that whoever believes in Him should not perish but have everlasting life" (John 3:16).
-   Second, it is not Jesus' resurrection or His being taken up into heaven (Luke 24:51) that grants Him a divine nature; there have been others who have been resurrected (for example, "many bodies of the saints who had fallen asleep were raised; and coming out of the graves after His resurrection, they went into the holy city and appeared to many" (Mat 27:52-53)). Moreover, as noted above, Enoch and Elijah did not die but were rather taken up into heaven directly.
-   Third, what *does* make Jesus divine is his eternal nature. John writes that "[i]n the beginning was the Word, and the Word was with God, and the Word was God" (John 1:1). "The Word became flesh [through Jesus], and dwelt among us" (John 1:14). Jesus is the incarnation of the eternal Word, which has been with God since the beginning. That Jesus shares God's identity can be said of no other man or prophet of the Bible.

Unlike those who walked with God (Enoch), performed great miracles (Elijah) or were taken into heaven and spared death (Enoch and Elijah), Jesus is the "only begotten Son" (John 3:16).

5. The Trinity

a. *If the Father, Son and Holy Spirit Are All God, then Isn't Jesus the Father and the Holy Spirit?*

A basic rule of logic is that: If A = C; and if B = C; then A = C. Applying logic to the Trinity, does it not mean that: If Jesus = God; and if the Father = God; then Jesus = the Father?

The problem here is the definition of "=." If it means fully identical and coterminous, in a mathematical sense, then Jesus does not = God. But if it means, "Jesus *is* God," with all the ontological depth of the word "is," then that statement is correct. Jesus is God in his essence, and Son in his person; the Father is God in his essence, and Father in his person; the Holy Spirit is God in his essence, and *Paraclete* in his person.

Trinitarian theology does not hold that Jesus = God in the identical and coterminous sense. The conclusion drawn above is therefore false according to Trinitarian theology. But this does not mean that Trinitarian theology is contradictory, since the conclusion was reached using at least one premise that is false according to Trinitarian theology.

No biblical verses state whether Jesus was God in the coterminous (identical) sense or only in essence. But given that the Bible gives certain attributes to Jesus that God does not hold (*e.g.*, Jesus died on the cross) and certain attributes to God that Jesus does not hold (*e.g.*, God is a Trinity), it is clear that God is not Jesus in the coterminous sense. Otherwise, we would have to conclude that Jesus is a Trinity and Jesus sent his Son to die on the cross.

Therefore, Jesus and the Father are God in the ontological but not coterminous sense. The conclusion ("Jesus = the Father") is not true, not because the Syllogism is invalid, but rather, because the premises ("Jesus = God" and "the Father = God") are not true in the identical and coterminous sense.

b. *How Could Jesus be God if He Worshipped God as Any Other Mortal?*

Dr. Baagil asks: "How could Jesus be God if he worshiped God as any other mortal (Luke 5:16): 'And he withdrew himself into the wilderness, and prayed'" (p. 40).

It is true that according to Luke 5:16, Jesus "withdrew himself in the deserts, and prayed." It is important to first note that Christ has two natures (and likewise, two wills) united in His one person. So, while Christ's divinity is in constant communion with God the Father and the Holy Spirit, Christ's humanity still must pray. One can see this in the Garden of Gethsemane, where Christ's human nature, naturally wishing to have "this cup" taken from him, prays in order for His human will to remain subjected to the will of God.

Prayer and communing, like love, imply a bidirectional activity that must involve at least two persons / entities. Therefore, we can see that there is one God even though Jesus prayed to God because it was Jesus' human nature that prayed to God.

c. Pagan Influence on the Doctrine of the Trinity and Christian Practices

Dr. Baagil writes: "No doubt Roman paganism had influence in this doctrine, the triune god; Sabbath was shifted to Sunday; December 25, which was the birthday of their sun-god Mithra, was introduced as Jesus' birthday, although the Bible clearly predicted and forbade the decoration of Christmas trees in Jeremiah 10:2-5: "Thus saith the Lord, Learn not the way of the heathen, and be not dismayed at the signs of heaven; for the heathen are dismayed at them. For the customs of the people are vain: for one cutteth a tree out of the forest, the work of the hands of the workman, with the axe. They deck it with silver and with gold, they fasten it with nails and with hammers, that it move not. They are upright as the palm tree, but speak not: they must needs be borne, because they cannot go. Be not afraid of them; for they cannot do evil, neither also is in them to do good" (p. 29).

We will explore each of the concerns raised by Dr. Baagil in the following order: (i) Christian worship on Sunday; (ii) Christmas on December 25 as pagan Mithra worship; and (iii) the prohibition of decorating Christmas trees.

i. Christian Worship on Sunday

(1) Overview

Dr. Baagil states that the "Sabbath was shifted to Sunday" (p. 29). As with his argument as to the doctrine of the Trinity, Dr. Baagil does not actually provide any evidence that paganism is the source of Christian Sunday worship. In any event, his argument mixes up two distinct points. While it is true that God finished His work of creation and rested on the seventh day (Gen 2:2) and commanded the people of Israel to "remember the Sabbath day and keep it holy" (Exo 20:8), he never prohibited Sunday fellowship and worship. It is entirely possibly for a person to rest on the seventh day and then gather together for fellowship and worship on Sunday. There is nothing incompatible with these two concepts.

(2) Sabbath Blessing Extended to the Gentiles as Sunday Worship

The early Christian church was comprised of both Jews and Gentiles. Many early Christians were thus Gentiles not familiar with the Hebrew law and the commandment to keep the Sabbath (the seventh day) as the day of rest. Moreover, Jesus states in Mark 2:27-28 and Luke 6:5 that He is "Lord even of the Sabbath," which they interpret to mean that he has the power to change the Sabbath to a different day. Many Christians have therefore changed the Sabbath to Sunday, which they feel symbolically represents the acceptance of Christ as Messiah and broadens blessing and redemption to all of the Gentiles, who may not be bound by the Jewish law. This does not counter the commandment to keep the Sabbath, because in their view, the spirit of this commandment is to give one day to God; whether that day is the first or the seventh is immaterial to the greater purpose of the commandment.

Christian Sunday worship and communion can be traced back as early as Acts 20, where Paul and the believers came together for communion on the first day of the week (Sunday) (Acts 20:7). Thus, as testified in the Scriptures, the early Church chose Sunday worship because it marks a shift from the old covenant to the new. The Jews traditionally worshipped on the eve of the Sabbath, but Christians now honored God on the first day of the week because it was on that day that Christ rose from the dead. This gives God special dominion as Christians begin each new week with worship and remember resurrection in the tomb early on the Sunday morning, following the crucifixion.

(3) The Place of Conscience in Celebrating the Sabbath

Is Christian Sunday worship prohibited by the Scripture? We should remember that in the New Covenant, we are no longer bound by strict legalism but rather by the law of grace. The Apostle Paul writes that "One man esteems one day above another: another esteems every day alike. Let each man be fully assured in his own mind. He that regards the day, regards it unto the Lord; he that does not regard the day, does not regard it unto the Lord; and he that eats, eats unto the Lord, for he gives God thanks; and he that eats not, unto the Lord he eats not, and gives God thanks" (Rom 14:5-6). The key is thus that each person be fully convinced in his own heart that his choice is right, and "not to let anyone judge you by .. a Sabbath day. [This is] a shadow of the things that were to come; the reality, however, is found in Christ" (Col 2:16-17)

ii. Christmas on December 25 as Pagan Worship

Dr. Baagil writes that "December 25, which was the birthday of their sun-god Mithra, was introduced as Jesus' birthday" (p. 29). There are several problems with this argument. First, Dr. Baagil fails to provide any evidence that December 25 was a day dedicated to the pagan god Mithra or that the Christians came to celebrate the birth of Jesus on December 25 because that day was already dedicated to a pagan festival. Second, even if paganism were shown to be the underlying reason for December 25 being selected as the birthday of Christ, the following problems would arise in Dr. Baagil's argument:

- The day is not dedicated to pagan worship. On December 25, Christians worship Jesus, whom they believe to be the incarnation of the one and only God, not the pagan sun god Mithra.
- Early Christians were aggressively persecuted. The early church was trying to survive in a pagan-dominated world. If they were to choose a pagan festival to commemorate the birth of Christ, it would be in order to blend into local celebrations and avoid attracting the attention of their persecutors, not because they were actually engaging in the worship of the pagan god.
- The Church is charged with the task of reshaping culture, and redeeming even pagan holidays when introducing Christ to them. Thus, if early Christians choose the day of celebration of the pagan sun god Mithra to worship Jesus, this would simply

be one example of how Christ came to take dominion over all idolatrous activities and redeemed them. What was initially destined for pagan worship was redeemed when it was taken over by worship to the one true God. The Church did no wrong but to bring to local practices in line with the worship of the one true God.

What is key to all of this is not the exact day on which Christ was born, but rather, the hearts of the Christians actually participating in Christmas celebrations: these Christians are participating in the celebration of Christ, not of a pagan god.

Yet even if a Pagan holiday were adopted by Christians to celebrate the birth of Christ, and such adoption could not be justified by, for example, the conversion of former pagan worship into worship of God, this still would not undermine Christianity because the adoption of traditions by Christians or churches does not invalidate the authority of the Bible or Christian doctrine recorded in the Bible, the Ecumenical Councils or other authorities.

iii. Prohibition of Decorating Christmas Trees

Dr. Baagil argues that "the Bible clearly predicted and forbade the decoration of Christmas trees in Jeremiah 10:2-5: 'Thus saith the Lord, Learn not the way of the heathen, and be not dismayed at the signs of heaven; for the heathen are dismayed at them. For the customs of the people are vain: for one cutteth a tree out of the forest, the work of the hands of the workman, with the axe. They deck it with silver and with gold, they fasten it with nails and with hammers, that it move not. They are upright as the palm tree, but speak not: they must needs be borne, because they cannot go. Be not afraid of them; for they cannot do evil, neither also is in them to do good'" (p. 29).

A close reading of Jeremiah 10:2-5 will however clearly show that what is being discussed is a wooden idol (*i.e.*, a material effigy that is worshipped), not a Christmas tree:

-   "The customs of the people are vain: for one cutteth a tree out of the forest, the work of the hands of the workman, with the axe" (Jer 10:3). The "work" is fashioned by a workman, sometimes translated as "craftsman" (*e.g.*, as in the NIV) with an axe, sometimes as "chisel" (*e.g.*, as in the NIV). The idea here is that the wood of the tree that is cut down is fashioned by a workman using an axe or chisel. The generally accepted interpretation is that the trees are made into wooden idols, and this interpretation is consistent with the rest of Jeremiah 10, which condemns idolatrous "gods" (*see, e.g.*, Jer 10:8, which says "wooden idols" are "worthless" and Jer 10:11, which states that the false gods will "perish"). This fashioning of wood into idols does not occur with Christmas trees, which are simply cut down and erected in homes.

- "They deck it with silver and with gold" (Jer 10:4). After the pagan tree is cut down and fashioned into an idol, it is beautified with precious metals such as silver and gold. While it is true that Christmas trees are decorated with tinsel, lights and ornaments, they are not traditionally decorated with silver and gold.

- "They are upright as the palm tree, but speak not: they must needs be borne, because they cannot go. Be not afraid of them; for they cannot do evil, neither also is it in them to do good" (Jer 10:5). This verse very clearly points to the fact that what is being condemned are idols. The pagan traditionally fashion idols out of wood, metal or other materials. The idols are given human form, with eyes, mouths and feet, yet, as this verse points out, the idols are futile, because they cannot speak, move or do any good or evil. "Palm trees" is frequently translated as "scare crow" (*see, e.g.*, the NIV, ESV and ISV translations), which further reinforces the fact that what is being discussed is given human likeness, but has no life in it. Again, Christmas trees fall outside of this category because they are not given any human likeness.

- "There is none like you, O Lord; you are great, and your name is great in might." (Jer 10:6). This once again reinforces the fact that what is being condemned are idols because they seek to compete with and take true worship away from Jehovah, the one true God and the only God worthy of worship.

- "They are both stupid and foolish; the instruction of idols is but wood!" (Jer 10:8). This verse makes crystal clear the context and meaning of Jeremiah 10:3-4: what is being referenced are wooden idols, not Christmas trees.

- "Beaten silver is brought from Tarshish, and gold from Uphaz. They are the work of the craftsman and of the hands of the goldsmith; their clothing is violet and purple; they are all the work of skilled men" (Jer 10:9). False idols are dressed in blue and purple to make them look regal.

- "But the LORD is the true God" (Jer 10:10). This verse contrasts what has been discussed theretofore—false idols—with the one true God.
- "The gods who did not make the heavens and the earth shall perish from the earth and from under the heavens" (Jer 10:11). This verse gives the final destination and end of false idols—destruction.
- "Every man is stupid and without knowledge; every goldsmith is put to shame by his idols, for his images are false, and there is no breath in them" (Jer 10:14). This verse seals the meaning of Jeremiah 10. Those who make idols are to be shamed, for they are the craftsmen of false images.

In conclusion, Jeremiah 10:3-4 should not be read to refer to Christmas trees, but rather, to wooden idols fashioned out of trees and then falsely worship by idolaters. Yet even if it *did* refer to Christmas trees, the modern practice of using Christmas trees still would not undermine the validity of Christianity or of the Bible; it would simply mean that some modern Christians has come to adopt a tradition that contravenes biblical standards.

d. The Doctrine of the Trinity

Dr. Baagil attacks the doctrine of the Trinity throughout his book. He first asserts that paganism is at the root of the doctrine: "No doubt Roman paganism had influence in this doctrine, the triune god" (p. 29). He does not actually provide any evidence that paganism is the source of the doctrine of the Trinity, but he does argue that the one biblical reference to the Trinity is an addition to the Scripture by the authors of the King James Version of the Bible and that the doctrine has no place in the actual, unadulterated Bible.

We will examine this claim below and then refute additional points that Dr. Baagil argues against the doctrine of the Trinity.

i. Overview: the King James Version "Addition"

Dr. Baagil devotes a section to the book on the Christian doctrine of the Trinity. He attacks the doctrine by pointing out that the verse that is sometimes used to justify the Trinity—"For there are three that bear witness in heaven: the Father, the Word, and the Holy Spirit; and these three are one" (1Jn 5:7)—does not exist in some translations of the Bible. Dr. Baagil writes that the verse is in the King James Version, but was "expunged in the Revised Standard Version of 1952 and 1971 and in many other Bibles, as it was a gloss that had encroached on the Greek text" (p. 28). Dr. Baagil further points to the fact that the verse does not exist in the New American Standard Bible.

In fact, Dr. Baagil is correct: 1 John 5:7, as recorded in the King James Version of the Bible, is not recorded in most other English translations. It is recorded in the New King James Version, because the New King James Version was based on the King James Version. However, it is not contained in the other English translations, including the American Standard Version, Revised Standard Version, Bible in Basic English, New International Version and International Standard Version.

The reason the translators of these latter versions did not include the King James Version's reference to the "Father, the Word, and the Holy Spirit" is this language is not found in any Greek manuscripts or New Testament translation prior to the 16th century. Wishing to remain faithful to the earliest available manuscripts, the translators of these latter versions removed the language introduced by the King James Version.

For the reader's convenience, following is a table summarizing how several English translations of the Bible render 1 John 5:7 and its surrounding verses:

Verse	KJV	ASV	RSV	BBE	NKJV	NIV	ISV
This is He who came by water and blood-- Jesus Christ; not only by water, but by water and blood.	1Jn 5:6	1Jn 5:6	1Jn 5:6	1Jn 5:6	1Jn 5:6	1Jn 5:6	1Jn 5:6
And it is the Spirit who bears witness, because the Spirit is truth.	" "	1Jn 5:7	1Jn 5:7	1Jn 5:7	" "	" "	" "
For there are three that bear witness in	1Jn 5:7	na	na	na	1Jn 5:7	na	na

heaven: the Father, the Word, and the Holy Spirit; and these three are one.							
And there are three that bear witness [on earth]:	1Jn 5:8	1Jn 5:8	1Jn 5:8	1Jn 5:8	1Jn 5:8	1Jn 5:7	1Jn 5:7
the Spirit, the water, and the blood; and these three agree as one.	" "	" "	" "	" "	" "	1Jn 5:8	1Jn 5:8
If we receive the witness of men, the witness of God is greater; for this is the witness of God which He has testified of His Son.	1Jn 5:9	1Jn 5:9	1Jn 5:9	1Jn 5:9	1Jn 5:9	1Jn 5:9	1Jn 5:9

ii. History and Development of the Doctrine of the Trinity

While it is true that the King James Version therefore introduces language into 1 John 5:7 that does not exist in the earliest extant New Testament manuscripts, one cannot conclude, as Dr. Baagil does, that "the Trinity is not Biblical. The word Trinity is not even in the Bible or Bible dictionaries, was never taught by Jesus and was never mentioned by him. There is no basis or proof in the Bible whatsoever for the acceptance of the Trinity" (p. 28).

It is true that the doctrine of the Trinity was not formally universally recognized by the Church until the First Council of Constantinople of 381 (the second Ecumenical Council), where in their "Letter of the bishops gathered in Constantinople," the sacred synod of orthodox bishops recognized "the uncreated and consubstantial and co-eternal Trinity." However, while not formally recognized by the church in a universal manner prior to this Council, the doctrine existed since the very beginnings of the Church.

For example, before the second Ecumenical Council, St. Athanasius, the twentieth bishop of Alexandria, issued one of the primary creeds of the early church. It states that "the catholic faith is this: That we worship one God in Trinity, and Trinity in Unity."

iii. Is There a Biblical Basis for the Doctrine of the Trinity?

While the Bible does not explicitly reference the Trinity by name, it does teach that while the Father is God, the Son is God and the Holy Spirit is God, there is only one God. Therefore, God is one and triune; he exists in three persons, as the doctrine of the Trinity holds.

(1) One God

The Old Testament explicitly states that there is only one God:

- Deu 4:35 Unto thee it was showed, that thou mightest know that Jehovah he is God; there is none else besides him.
- Deu 4:39 Know therefore this day, and lay it to thy heart, that Jehovah he is God in heaven above and upon the earth beneath; there is none else.
- Deu 32:39 See now that I, even I, am he, And there is no god with me.
- 2Sa 22:32 For who is God, save Jehovah? And who is a rock, save our God?
- Isa 37:20 Now therefore, O Jehovah our God, save us from his hand, that all the kingdoms of the earth may know that thou art Jehovah, even thou only.
- Isa 43:10 Ye are my witnesses, saith Jehovah, and my servant whom I have chosen; that ye may know and believe me, and understand that I am he: before me there was no God formed, neither shall there be after me.
- Isa 44:6 Thus saith Jehovah, the King of Israel, and his Redeemer, Jehovah of hosts: I am the first, and I am the last; and besides me there is no God.
- Isa 45:5 I am Jehovah, and there is none else; besides me there is no God. I will gird thee, though thou hast not known me;
- Isa 45:14 Thus saith Jehovah ... there is none else, there is no God.
- Isa 46:9 Remember the former things of old: for I am God, and there is none else; I am God, and there is none like me.

This is also affirmed in the New Testament.

- John 5:44   How can you believe, who receive honor from one another, and do not seek the honor that comes from the only God?
- Rom 3:30   there is one God who will justify the circumcised by faith and the uncircumcised through faith.
- Gal 3:20   Now a mediator does not mediate for one only, but God is one.
- Eph 4:6   one God and Father of all, who is above all, and through all, and in you al
- 1Ti 1:17   Now to the King eternal, immortal, invisible, to God who alone is wise, be honor and glory forever and ever.
- 1Ti 2:5   For there is one God and one Mediator between God and men, the Man Christ Jesus,
- Jam 2:19   You believe that there is one God. You do well.
- Jud 1:25   To God our Savior, Who alone is wise, Be glory and majesty, Dominion and power.

The Scriptures further teach that there is none like God:

- Exo 9:14   for at this time I will send all My plagues to your very heart, and on your servants and on your people, that you may know that there is none like Me in all the earth.
- 1Ch 17:20   O LORD, there is none like You, nor is there any God besides You, according to all that we have heard with our ears.
- Isa 44:8   Do not fear, nor be afraid; Have I not told you from that time, and declared it? You are My witnesses. Is there a God besides Me? Indeed there is no other Rock; I know not one.' "

And moreover, that there is only one true God:

- 2Ch 15:3   For a long time Israel has been without the true God
- Jer 10:10   But the LORD is the true God; He is the living God and the everlasting King.
- John 17:3   And this is eternal life, that they may know You, the only true God, and Jesus Christ whom You have sent.
- 1Th 1:9   you turned to God from idols to serve the living and true God
- 1Jn 5:20   And we know that the Son of God has come and has given us an understanding, that we may know Him who is true;

and we are in Him who is true, in His Son Jesus Christ. This is the true God and eternal life.

All other "gods" are false gods (idols):

- Psa 96:5   For all the gods of the peoples are idols, But the LORD made the heavens.
- Jer 5:7   "How shall I pardon you for this? Your children have forsaken Me And sworn by those that are not gods.
- Jer 16:20   Will a man make gods for himself, Which are not gods?
- 1Co 8:4   we know that an idol is nothing in the world, and that there is no other God but one.

(2) The Father is God

The Scriptures explicitly state that the Father of Jesus is God:

- John 17:3   And this is eternal life, that they may know You, the only true God, and Jesus Christ whom You have sent.
- 1Co 8:6   yet for us there is one God, the Father, of whom are all things, and we for Him; and one Lord Jesus Christ, through whom are all things, and through whom we live.

This is further reinforced by the recurring expression *"God and Father* of our Lord Jesus Christ":

- 2Co 1:3   Blessed be the God and Father of our Lord Jesus Christ, the Father of mercies and God of all comfort.
- Eph 1:3   Blessed be the God and Father of our Lord Jesus Christ, who has blessed us with every spiritual blessing in the heavenly places in Christ.
- 1Pe 1:3   Blessed be the God and Father of our Lord Jesus Christ, who according to His abundant mercy has begotten us again to a living hope through the resurrection of Jesus Christ from the dead.

(3) The Son is God

The Scriptures explicitly state that Jesus Christ is God. The New Testament declares:

- John 1:1   In the beginning was the Word, and the Word was with God, and *the Word was God.*

-   Acts 20:28: "the church of God which He purchased with His own blood." The church of God was purchased with God's own blood. Since it was Jesus' blood that was shed, we can conclude that Jesus is God.
-   Tit 2:13 our great *God* and Savior *Jesus Christ*.
-   "Our God and Savior Jesus Christ" or "our Lord and Savior Jesus Christ" is also mentioned in 2Pe 1:1; 1:11; 2:20; 3:2, 18.
-   Heb 1:8 to the Son He says: "your throne, o God, is forever and ever."
-   1Jn 5:20 we are in Him who is true, in His Son Jesus Christ. This is the true God and eternal life.

The Old Testament prophesied that the Messiah would be God: "For unto us a Child is born, Unto us a Son is given; And the government will be upon His shoulder. And His name will be called Wonderful, Counselor, *Mighty God*" (Isa 9:6).

Moreover, Jesus has titles belonging only to God:

-   Isa 44:6 "Thus says the LORD, the King of Israel, And his *Redeemer*, the LORD of hosts: 'I am *the First and I am the Last*; Besides Me there is no God.
-   Rev 1:17 He laid His right hand on me, saying to me, "Do not be afraid; I am *the First and the Last*.
-   1Ti 6:15 He who is the blessed and only Potentate, the *King of kings and Lord of lords*.
-   Rev 17:14 *He is Lord of lords* and *King of kings*.

Jesus receive honors, prayer and worship due to God alone:

-   John 5:23 that all should honor the Son just as they honor the Father. He who does not honor the Son does not honor the Father who sent Him.
-   John 14:14 If you ask anything in My name, I will do it.
-   Heb 1:6 But when He again brings the firstborn into the world, He says: "let all the angels of God worship him."

For the Jews, it was clear that Jesus claimed to be God. This is why they accused him of blasphemy: "The Jews answered Him, saying, 'For a good work we do not stone You, but for blasphemy, and because You, being a Man, make Yourself God'" (John 10:33). They tried to stone Jesus (the penalty for blasphemy) for invoking the Divine Name upon Himself (John 8:58-59).

Dr. Baagil also recognizes that the Bible teaches that Jesus is God, for he quotes John 1:1 ("In the beginning was the Word, and the Word was with God, and the Word was God"). However, Dr. Baagil, misunderstanding the meaning of the Trinity, concludes that Jesus' being God means that there must be "at least" two Gods (p. 34), which is in turn a contradiction of the oneness of God as related in many passages in the Bible (p. 34):

> (Deuteronomy 4:39): ". . . that the Lord he is God in heaven above, and upon the earth beneath: there is none else"; (Deuteronomy 6:4): "Hear, O Israel: The Lord our God is one Lord"; (Isaiah 43:10-11): ". . . that ye may know and believe me, and understand that I am He: before me there was no God formed, neither shall there be after me. I, even I, am the Lord; and beside me there is no saviour"; (Isaiah 44:6): "Thus with the Lord ... I am the first, and I am the last; and beside me there is no God"; (Isaiah 45:18): "For thus with the Lord that created the heavens; God himself that formed the earth and made it; he hath established it, he created it not in vain, he formed ii to be inhabited: I am the Lord; and there is none else."

Dr. Baagil fundamentally misunderstands that the doctrine of the Trinity holds both that God is one *in three persons*. The mystery of the Trinity is that the Father is God, the Son is God and the Holy Spirit is God, and yet God is one.

(4) The Holy Spirit is God

The Holy Spirit is equated with God throughout the Scriptures:

- Acts 5:3 But Peter said, "Ananias, why has Satan filled your heart to lie to the Holy Spirit and keep back part of the price of the land for yourself? Acts 5:4 While it remained, was it not your own? And after it was sold, was it not in your own control? Why have you conceived this thing in your heart? You have not lied to men but to God."
- 2Co 3:17 Now the Lord is the Spirit.

Moreover, the Holy Spirit has the incommunicable attributes of God: the Holy Spirit is eternal (Heb 9:14), omnipresent (Psa 139:7-8) and omniscient (1Co 2:10-11).

Finally, the Holy Spirit is involved in the works of God: the creation (Gen 1:2), incarnation (Mat 1:18, 20) and resurrection (Rom 1:4).

(5) The Father, the Son, and the Holy Spirit Are Distinct Persons

(a) Overview

That the Father, the Son, and the Holy Spirit are distinct persons is most clearly manifested at the baptism of Jesus, when each member of the Trinity was present in a different form: the Father as the voice in heaven, the Son as Jesus and the Holy Spirit as the dove: "When He had been baptized, Jesus came up immediately from the water; and behold, the heavens were opened to Him, and He saw the Spirit of God descending like a dove and alighting upon Him. And suddenly a voice came from heaven, saying, 'This is My beloved Son, in whom I am well pleased'" (Mat 3:16-17).

This is further clarified by the Great Commission, where Jesus instructed the disciples to "make disciples of all the nations, baptizing them in the name of the Father and of the Son and of the Holy Spirit" (Mat 28:19). If the Father, the Son and the Holy Spirit were all the same person, then it would have sufficed to have merely listed one of them.

(b) Jesus is not the Father

The Scriptures repeatedly refer to Jesus and the Father as two distinct persons. For example, Ephesians 1:3 blesses "the God and Father of our Lord Jesus Christ, who has blessed us with every spiritual blessing in the heavenly places in Christ."

It is true that Jesus says, "I and My Father are one" (John 10:30). However, Jesus did not say that "I am my Father" or that "I and My Father are one person." Rather, he said that they were "one," in the sense that they had essential though not personal unity. This is made clear by the use of the first person plural *esmen* ("are") implying two distinct persons.

This is further clarified by the use of "one" in John 17:21, where Jesus, referring to "those whom You [the Father] have given Me" (John 17:9), prays that they may be one." Of course, it would be illogical to conclude that Jesus means by this that the disciples would be one person; rather, he means that they would have essential unity, "as You, Father, are in Me, and I in You" (John 17:21). His prayer is that the disciples "may be one in Us, that the world may believe that You sent Me" (John 17:21). This does not of course mean that each disciple would become a part of the Godhead.

Jesus further states that "He who has seen Me has seen the Father" (John 14:9). Again, Jesus does not state that He and the Father are the same person. Rather, he is stating that one sees the Father *in* Jesus because He and the Father share the same essence. They are each distinct persons in the Trinity who share the same nature. Note that Jesus does not state that "I am the Father," but rather, "I am *in* the Father" (John 14:10) (italics added).

Colossians states that in Jesus "dwells all the fullness of the Godhead bodily" (Col 2:9). However, while the fullness of the Godhead dwells bodily in Jesus, Jesus is not the Godhead, for the Godhead also consists of the Father and Holy Spirit.

(c) Jesus is not the Holy Spirit

Jesus says that He "will pray the Father, and He will give you another Helper, that He may abide with you forever" (John 14:16). This "Helper" is the Holy Spirit, as clarified in John 15:26: "when the Helper comes, whom I shall send to you from the Father, the Spirit of truth who proceeds from the Father, He will testify of Me." The Holy Spirit is not Jesus because the Holy Spirit "will glorify [Jesus], for He will take of what is [Jesus'] and declare it to you" (John 16:14).

The distinction between Jesus and the Holy Spirit is further clarified at the baptism of Jesus, when the Spirit of God descended like a dove and alighted upon Him (Mat 3:16).

(d) The Father is not the Holy Spirit

The Father gives the Holy Spirit ("I will pray the Father, and He will give you another Helper" (John 14:16)). This "Helper" is the Holy Spirit (*i.e.*, the "Spirit of truth who proceeds from the Father" (John 15:26)). Moreover, the Holy Spirit makes intercession with the Father: "the Spirit Himself makes intercession for us with groanings which cannot be uttered. Now He who searches the hearts knows what the mind of the Spirit is, because He makes intercession for the saints according to the will of God" (Rom 8:26-27).

(6) Conclusion: A Triune God

Because the Scripture teaches that there is one God, and yet the Father, Son and Holy Spirit are God, one can conclude that God is in three persons.

6. Was Jesus Crucified?

a. The "Hearsay" of the disciples, Apostles and Other Witnesses Ought Not be Trusted

Dr. Baagil asks the reader, "Do you give more weight to what Jesus said or to hearsay of the disciples, apostles and other witnesses?" (p. 44), completely missing the inherent contradiction in labeling the testimony of witnesses as "hearsay."

"Hearsay," as commonly defined in legal contexts where it is most often invoked, is any statement, other than one made by a declarant while testifying, offered as evidence to prove the truth of the matter asserted. For example, if a declarant, in order to prove that a thief stole a vehicle, offers as evidence of the theft the statement made by the declarant's neighbor that the neighbor saw the thief steal the vehicle, the statement would be classified as hearsay. However, if the declarant himself states that he saw the thief steal the car, such a statement would not qualify as hearsay because the declarant himself witnessed the event and is not offering up someone else's statement as evidence of the theft.

The contradiction in Dr. Baagil's statement is thus that, on the one hand, he characterizes the testimony of disciples and apostles as "hearsay"; yet on the other hand, by use of the qualifier "other," he recognizes them as "witnesses." Dr. Baagil thus attempts to undermine the credibility of eye witness accounts of the crucifixion, including Matthew, a former tax collector who was called by Jesus to be one of the twelve disciples and the author of the Gospel of Matthew, and John, a disciple of Jesus, possibly the youngest of His twelve disciples, and the author of the Gospel of John. The statements of such writers who witnessed the events in question cannot be classified as "hearsay."

b. Jesus' Prophecy about His Death Should Not Be Read Literally; Jesus Only Meant He Would "Suffer"

At this point in the book, the Christian protests: "But Jesus himself said that he will rise from the dead (Luke 24:46): 'And said unto them, Thus it is written, and thus it behooved Christ to suffer, and to rise

from the dead the third day'" (p. 44). For Dr. Baagil, however, Jesus'
prediction of his "death" should not be read literally. He writes,
"Suffering is often exaggerated in the Bible and termed "dead" as Paul
said (I Corinthians 15:31): 'I protest by your rejoicing which I have in
Christ, I die daily' (*i.e.*, I suffer daily)" (p. 44).

Of course, Dr. Baagil is correct in pointing out that by "I die
daily," Paul was speaking in a figurative sense (1Co 15:31). Man is
given only one body, and no man has died more than once, never mind
on a daily basis. However, it would be wrong to conclude from this
that every reference to "death" in the Bible is a figurative allusion.
Physical death is a very real thing in the Bible. For instance:

- God promised Adam and Eve that if they eat the fruit of the
  tree of knowledge, "death" would come to them (Gen 2:17).
  The death that followed was not figurative suffering, but
  physical death
- When Cain attacked his brother Abel, he put him to death, not
  figuratively, but physically (Gen 4:8).
- When Pharaoh commanded the midwives to put the sons of the
  Hebrew women to death (Exo 1:16), he did not mean to merely
  cause them suffering. Of course, the intent of sending the infant
  sons of the Hebrew women into the river (Exo 1:22) was to
  cause them to drown, not merely to cause them pain.
- The same is of course true for the New Testament. For
  example, Matthew writes that an angel of the Lord came in a
  dream to Joseph, who was hiding from Herod with Mary and
  Jesus in Egypt, saying that it was safe to return to Israel
  because Herod was dead (Mat 2:19-20). Of course, the angel
  did not mean that Herod was in a state of suffering; rather, he
  meant that Herod was no more, and was thus no longer a threat
  to the child's life.

The question before us is then, when Jesus predicted his death in
Luke 24:46, did he mean his physical death or mere suffering, as Paul
used the term "death" in 1Co 15:31? The answer becomes clear by
examining Jesus' other predictions about his death:

- Jesus specifically predicts his death by crucifixion in Matthew:
  "After two days is the Passover, and the Son of man will be
  given up to the death of the cross" (Mat 26:2). Crucifixion was
  not a means of merely punishing by imposing suffering; it was

a method of imposing physical death. Roman soldiers did not take the condemned down from their crosses after they have sufficiently suffered and then let them go free. Rather, they confirmed that the condemned were dead or otherwise broke their legs (see John 19:31-32). Crucifixion was thus in Roman times the equivalent of a death sentence.

- Jesus also predicts the resurrection on the third day and that He would be "given cruel blows and put to death, and on the third day he will come back to life" (Luke 18:33). Coming back to life implies first having died. One does not come "back" to life if all he only suffered physically but never died.

c. *Jesus Prayed that God Deliver Jesus from the Cross; God Granted Jesus' Petition*

Dr. Baagil notes Jesus' words in Luke 22:42: "Father, if it is your will, take this cup from me; nevertheless, not my will, but yours, be done." Then, on the cross, he beseeched God, saying, "My God, my God, why have you forsaken me?" (Mat 27:46). Dr. Baagil interprets these words as prayers to be spared of the crucifixion (p. 44). Moreover, he writes that Jesus' pray to be spared was answered by God according to Luke, Hebrews and James:

- *Luke.* "An angel from heaven came to him, to give Jesus strength" (Luke 22:43), which for Baagil means that "an angel assured him that God would not leave him helpless." Nothing in the verse, however, suggests that God abandoned the plan of the crucifixion and removed Jesus therefrom. It merely states that an angel strengthened Jesus; in other words, that the angel helped Jesus to get through the last moments before his arrest, trial and crucifixion.

- *Hebrews.* "Who in the days of his flesh, having sent up prayers and requests with strong crying and weeping to him who was able to give him salvation from death, had his prayer answered because of his fear of God" (Heb 5:7). This again does not mean that Jesus was spared of the cross. Jesus' prayer in Luke 22:42 was: "Father, *if it is your will*, take this cup from me; nevertheless, not my will, but yours, be done." It was *not* God's will that the cup be taken from Jesus, for it has been God's plan of salvation from the beginning that the Messiah be put to death (see, *e.g.*, the prophecies at Isa 53:7 (men were cruel to him, but he was gentle and quiet, like a lamb taken to its slaughter); Psa 22:16-18 (wounds would be made in his hands and feet and his clothes would be divided by chance); Zec 12:10 (Jesus' side would be pierced); Psa 34:20 (his bones would not be broken); etc.) and that this death would be for the salvation of the world (see, *e.g.*, the prophecies of Isa 53:8 ("He was taken from prison and from judgment, and who gave a thought to his fate? He was cut off from the land of the living: He came to his death for the sin of my people"); Dan 9:26 ("After the sixty-two weeks, the Messiah shall be cut off, but not for Himself"); John 1:29 ("John the Baptist saw Jesus coming to him and said, 'Behold, the Lamb of God, who takes away the sin of the world!'"); etc.). Because Jesus prayed that God's will be done, and God's will as prophesied throughout the Old Testament was salvation of the world through the sacrifice of the Messiah on the cross, the answer to Jesus' prayer was not sparing him of the cross but rather, strengthening and carrying Him through his trial and raising Him from the dead. While it is true, in accordance with Hebrews 5:7, that Jesus' prayer was answered, it was answered not in the way that Dr. Baagil interprets the prayer, but rather, in accordance with God's will for the sacrifice of Jesus and salvation of the world.

- *James.* "Pray for one another so that you may be made well. The fervent prayer of a righteous man avails much in its working" (Jam 5:16). Dr. Baagil once again interprets this to mean that Jesus' prayer in Luke 22:42 to "take this cup from me" was answered by God because Jesus was righteous. However, Dr. Baagil ignores the rest of Jesus' Luke 22:42 prayer: "nevertheless, not my will, but yours, be done." As already discussed above, God's will was for the sacrifice of the Messiah for the salvation of the world. Consider also John 3:16 ("For God so loved the world that He gave His only begotten Son, that whoever believes in Him should not perish but have everlasting life"), which further makes clear God's salvation plan. Therefore, because the prayers of a righteous man (Jesus) avail much, the only logical conclusion is that Jesus *was* crucified because such was the will of God that Jesus prayed for.

d. Jesus' Legs Were Not Broken; Therefore, He Was Not Crucified

Dr. Baagil's next point proves the very point he is arguing against: that Jesus *was* crucified. Baagil writes: "His legs were not broken by the Roman soldiers (John 19:32-33): 'Then came the soldiers, and brake the legs of the first, and of the other which was crucified with him. But when they came to Jesus, and saw that he was dead already, they brake not his legs.' Can you rely on these soldiers for pronouncing the death, or did they want to save Jesus as they found him innocent?" (p. 45).

Baagil concludes that the Roman soldiers did not break Jesus' legs, for they found He was already dead. However, their motivation in "finding" him dead was to save an innocent man. Therefore, they really found Him alive, but proceeded as though he were dead in order to save him.

The main problem with Dr. Baagil's argument is that on the one hand, he argues that Jesus was spared of crucifixion: He prayed that God deliver Him from the cross and God granted the petition. Yet here, he argues that Jesus *was* crucified and the soldiers that inspected him chose not to break His legs. Therefore, if Baagil is correct that the soldiers released Jesus from the cross before He died, then clearly Jesus *was* crucified, contrary to the *Qur'an*, which teaches that "they killed him not, nor crucified him, but so it was made to appear to them" (*Sura* 4, *ayah* 157-158).

A second problem with Dr. Baagil's argument is that it assumes that the soldiers would suddenly have a turn of heart and sympathize for Jesus, who was innocent, even though he presents no evidence to support such a view. Rather, the Scriptures paint a picture not of Roman soldiers who had mercy on Jesus, an innocent man, but rather, who severely abused Jesus. The whole garrison of soldiers (Mat 27:27) mocked Jesus by putting on him a purple robe (Mat 27:28) and crown of thorns. They bowed before Him and mocked Him, saying, Hail, King of the Jews! (Mat 27:29). They spat on Him and struck his head with a reed (Mat 27:30) and whipped him (John 19:1). Dr. Baagil offers no evidence to suggest that any members of this garrison had a change of heart and wished to show mercy on Jesus or that the soldiers that removed Jesus from the cross were not among the "entire garrison" (Mat 27:27) that abused Jesus.

e. No Blood Would Gush Out If Jesus Died on the Cross

i.   Would Jesus Bleed If He Were Dead?

Dr. Baagil then points to John 19:34 ("one of the soldiers made a wound in his side with a spear, and immediately blood and water came out") as evidence that Jesus did not die on the cross. He argues that if Jesus were already dead on the cross, blood and water would not have poured out of Jesus' side when it was pierced. Rather, "his blood would clot and no blood would gush out" (p. 45).

Here, Dr. Baagil is partly right in that the blood of a dead person clots. However, this is an eventual process; if a freshly killed body were pierced, the blood would still flow out. In the case of Jesus, he was not dead for a long time. The evidence is that the others that were crucified with Him were still alive, such that their legs were broken (John 19:32) to speed up asphyxiation. It is therefore likely that Jesus died shortly before that. His blood would still be in his veins in liquid form, though if he were left on the cross for a long time, blood and fluid would eventually pool in the legs and clot.

ii.   Why Did Blood and Water Flow Out?

Regarding the question as to why blood and water flowed out, several explanations have been presented. James Thompson, for example, "believed that Jesus did not die from exhaustion, the beatings or the 3 hours of crucifixion, but that he died from agony of mind producing rupture of the heart. His evidence comes from what happened when the Roman soldier pierced Christ's left side. The spear released a sudden flow of blood and water (John 19:34). Not only does this prove that Jesus was already dead when pierced, but Thompson believes it is also evidence of cardiac rupture. Respected physiologist Samuel Houghton believed that only the combination of crucifixion and rupture of the heart could produce this result" ("How did Jesus Christ die?" *ChristianAnswers.net*, available at <http://christiananswers.net/q-eden/jesusdeath.html>, last accessed on Aug. 23 2013.

Moreover, a medical doctor with a general practice who this author consulted confirmed that when a dead body is pierced at the side, more than just blood, including bile and other fluids, could come out of the side, depending on where exactly the body was pierced. It is possible that the New Testament evangelists, when writing of blood "and water," could be referring to these other fluids. Had it been Luke, the only evangelist who was a physician, rather than John, who recounted the piercing of the side, the event may have been described with more detail.

f. Jonah Was Alive in the Belly of the Whale; Therefore, Jesus was Alive in the Tomb

Dr. Baagil cites Jesus' prophecy with respect to Jonah and the whale: "As Jonah was three days and three nights in the belly of the whale, so will the Son of Man be three days and three nights in the heart of the earth" (Mat 12:40). Baagil first points out to the time discrepancy: "Disregard now the time factor [of Jesus in the grave], which was also not three days and three nights but one day (Saturday, daytime only) and two nights (Friday night and Saturday night)" (p. 45) and then concludes that because Jonah was "still alive when he was vomited out of the belly of the whale" (p. 45), Jesus was therefore "still alive as [Jesus] prophesied" (p. 46). Each of Dr. Baagil's two claims—the first with respect to the three days of timing and the second with respect to Jesus' having been alive in the tomb, will be treated in turn.

i. Was Jesus "Three Days and Three Nights in the Heart of the Earth"?

(1) Overview

Dr. Baagil points to Jesus' sign of his true mission when answering the Pharisees with the sign of Jonah: "For as [Jonah] was three days and three nights in the whale's belly, so shall the son of man be three days and three nights in the heart of the earth" (Mat 12:40). The author states that the time factor was off, since Jesus was not three days and three nights in the tomb, "but one day (Saturday, daytime only) and two nights (Friday night and Saturday night)" (p. 45).

(2) Part Validity to Dr. Baagil's Criticism

The Scriptures state that Jesus was crucified on Friday and was taken to the tomb late that evening, as the Sabbath was approaching:

> Mat 27:57 Now **when evening had come**, there came a rich man from Arimathea, named Joseph, who himself had also become a disciple of Jesus.
> Mark 15:42 Now **when evening had come**, because it was the Preparation Day, that is, the day before the Sabbath

> Luke 23:53 Then [Joseph] took [Jesus' body] down, wrapped it in linen, and laid it in a tomb that was hewn out of the rock, where no one had ever lain before. Luke 23:54 That day was the Preparation, and **the Sabbath drew near**.

Therefore, Jesus was not in the tomb during the day on Friday; he entered the tomb that evening.

The Scriptures then state that while it was still dark on Sunday morning, Jesus was no longer in the tomb:

> John 20:1 Now the first day of the week Mary Magdalene went to the tomb early, while it was still dark, and saw that the stone had been taken away from the tomb.

Therefore, the only *days* (excluding nights) that Jesus had only been in the tomb were Saturday (1 day) and for a few minutes on Friday just before sundown.

(3) Reconciliation

As a possible explanation, Pastor Doug from AmazingFacts.org argues that the "heart of the earth" is not the tomb, but rather, the "clutches" of the earth. He states that there is a major misconception regarding the "heart" of the earth. People assume it means the tomb, yet nowhere else in the Bible is the "heart" of the earth called the tomb.

When Jesus alluded to three days and three nights in the heart of the earth, He wasn't talking about the tomb or vault. He was talking about the heart of the earth meaning the clutches of the world. Every time the mob tried to destroy Jesus or stone Jesus or throw Him off a cliff through His whole Ministry, He was untouchable and walked right through their midst; they were never able to harm Him in any way because He was under God's protection. But on Thursday night in the Garden of Gethsemane when He said, "Now is the hour of darkness," He was arrested, beaten, and began suffering for the sins of the world.

He didn't start suffering for the sins of the world when He was on the Cross and the nails pierced His flesh; the suffering began in the Garden of Gethsemane, where He was taken from Pilate to Herod and back to Pilate again; to Caiaphas to Anna and back to Caiaphas, being dragged all over the place, beaten, mocked and whipped. He was a captive to the devil the same way Jonah was a captive to the whale.

He was in that dark, hopeless environment for three days and three nights the same way that Jesus was in the clutches of the lost world, for three days and three nights.

A problem with this explanation is it only explains how Jesus could be in the "heart of the earth" for two days (Friday and Saturday) and three nights (Thursday, Friday, and Saturday) only. However, the counting of time known as "inclusive reckoning," which counts any part of any day as a full day (as discussed by Amazingfacts.org[1]), can explain the discrepancy. Jesus makes this simple way of counting time crystal clear in Luke 13:32-33, where "today" is the first day, "tomorrow" is the second day, and the day after tomorrow is the third day.

Therefore, Jesus was in the "heart of the earth" for three nights (the Thursday of his arrest at Gethsamene, the Friday of his crucifixion at Golgotha and the Saturday in the tomb prior to his resurrection) and three days:

-   Friday (during the day) = Day 1
-   Sabbath (Jesus rested!) = Day 2
-   Sunday (eve/morning) = Day 3

In order to accept this interpretation, one must recognize that under the system of biblical inclusive reckoning, any part of one day is counted as the whole day.

ii. Was Jesus Alive in the Tomb?

As mentioned above, Dr. Baagil, based on Jesus' metaphor with respect to Jonah, concludes that Jesus never died on the cross but remained alive in the tomb, because just as Jonah "was three days and three nights in the belly of the whale, so will the Son of Man be three days and three nights in the heart of the earth" (Mat 12:40). The following problems undermine Dr. Baagil's reasoning:

-   Jesus' comparison to Jonah was a metaphor that does not mandate exact congruency. One should not thus demand a perfect match as to every element between things compared in Jesus' metaphor. Jesus never said that "just as Jonah was alive

---

[1]   See   http://www.amazingfacts.org/free-stuff/online-library/book-viewer.aspx?g=2770c1f2-5f00-43ee-a82e-46e7d14cc39f&l=en&t=Three%20Days%20and%20Three%20Nights.

in the belly of the whale for three days, so will I be alive in the grave." Jesus was instead making a comparison of the time factor (three days and three nights) and was referencing the broader lesson that just as the world lost hope in Jonah, who in the depths of the ocean three days and three nights, so too would the world lose hope in Jesus. Yet God had the power to raise Jesus and Jonah from the "depths of Sheol."

- It is not entirely clear whether Jonah was alive in the belly of the whale. The Scripture states that Jonah prayed to God "from the belly of the fish" (Jon 2:1) and "from the belly of Sheol" (Jon 2:2). Some interpret the fact that Jonah prayed to God from the belly of the whale as an indication that Jonah was alive in the belly of the whale; others interpret it to mean that his prayer was heard while he was physically in the belly of the whale, but that Jonah had already died and descended to Sheol (the underworld as referred to in the Old Testament). Per the latter interpretation, Jonah's soul was praying to God from the depths of Sheol. This is consistent with Jonah's prayer at 2:5: The waters surrounded me, even to my soul; the deep closed around me; weeds wrapped around my head (Jon 2:5). "Even to my soul" is an expression implying death. It would thus seem that Jonah sank towards the bottom of the ocean, into "the deep," before his dead body was swallowed up by the fish.

- Dr. Baagil's argument that Jesus never died is illogical in light of the fact that Jesus' disciple Joseph went to Pilate the evening of the crucifixion and asked for Jesus' body, which Pilate gave to him (Mat 27:57-58). When Joseph took the body, he wrapped it in a linen cloth (Mat 27:59) and laid it in the tomb and rolled a large stone against the door of the tomb (Mat 27:60). If Jesus indeed were indeed alive when he was taken by the cross, Joseph surely would have noticed Jesus' breathing and rejoiced. Rather than lay Jesus' body in the tomb, further locking it up behind a large stone without access to food and water, and thus further jeopardizing the state of Jesus' already precarious health after hours of hanging on the cross, Jesus would have immediately summoned for medical attention to help further strengthen Jesus' body.

- Mary Magdalene and the other Mary were present when Joseph laid Jesus' body at the tomb (Mat 27:61). Therefore, even if Joseph were completely oblivious to the fact that Jesus was breathing and still alive, there is a high chance that either Mary would have noticed and would have stopped Joseph from putting a living man in the tomb.

g. Jesus Stated that He Did Not Die on the Cross

Dr. Baagil writes, "Jesus himself stated that he didn't die on the cross. Early Sunday morning Mary Magdalene went to the sepulchre, which was empty. She saw somebody standing who looked like a gardener. She recognized him after conversation to be Jesus and wanted to touch him. Jesus said (John 20:17): "Touch me not; for I am not yet ascended to my Father. . :" "Touch me not," perhaps because the fresh wound would hurt him. "I am not yet ascended to my Father," means that he was still alive, not dead yet, because if somebody dies, then he goes back to the Creator. This was the strongest proof admitted by Jesus himself" (p. 45).

The error here is that it assumes that just because someone dies, he automatically ascends to the Father. This is not the case, and certainly was not the case for Jesus. As has been recited by Christians for centuries in the Apostles' Creed, after Jesus was crucified, died and was buried, he "descended into hell." Some believe that during the time in which Jesus' body was in the tomb, he descended into hell to preach the Gospel. Such a view would be in keeping with 1Pe 4:6 ("For this reason the gospel was preached also to those who are dead, that they might be judged according to men in the flesh, but live according to God in the spirit") and an interpretation of 1Pe 3:18-20 ("Christ also suffered once for sins, the just for the unjust, that He might bring us to God, being put to death in the flesh but made alive by the Spirit, by whom also He went and preached to the spirits in prison, who formerly were disobedient, when once the Divine longsuffering waited in the days of Noah, while the ark was being prepared, in which a few, that is, eight souls, were saved through water") by which Jesus offered salvation not only to all those who came after Him, but also those who came before and had already descended into hell.

It is therefore false that Jesus said that He did not die on the cross. Rather, He what He said is that He had not yet ascended to His father, which does not necessarily mean that He did not die on the cross.

h. Because Jesus Had a Body when He Appeared to the Disciples, He Could Not Have Died on the Cross

Dr. Baagil continues: "After the alleged crucifixion the disciples thought that he was not the same Jesus in body but spiritualized, because resurrected bodies are spiritualized" (p. 46). Moreover, Baagil cites Jesus' words in Luke: "The sons of this age marry and are given in marriage. But those who are counted worthy to attain that age, and the resurrection from the dead, neither marry nor are given in marriage; nor can they die anymore, for they are equal to the angels and are sons of God, being sons of the resurrection" (Luke 20:36). Dr. Baagil goes on to argue that because Jesus said that in the resurrection, the resurrected are "equal unto the angels," the resurrected will not have physical bodies (p. 46). Therefore, Jesus, who had a physical body, cannot be said to have resurrected.

Dr. Baagil's argument is flawed for the following reasons:

- He misinterprets Luke 20:36 as indicating that the resurrected are identical to the angels. Of course, this is not the case: The believers will be distinct from the angels. For example, they will judge the angels (1Co 6:3). What Jesus is saying is that the resurrected will be like the angels in one particular sense—the angels do not marry in heaven.

- Even if Jesus did mean that the believers will be like the angels in heaven in their physical manifestation, he fails to provide any evidence whatsoever that angels, unlike Jesus after His resurrection, do not have bodies. On the contrary, most of the biblical evidence indicates that angels *do* have bodies:
  o Angels throughout the Scripture are described in physical terms. The detailed descriptions of their appearances imply that they have bodies.
  o The Seraph (*pl.*, Seraphim) is a six-winged creature (Isa 6:1).
  o The Cherub (*pl.*, Cherubim) has four faces, four wings and hands like those of a man (Eze 10:8, 21).
  o The Four Living Creatures are covered in eyes, each with six wings (Rev 4:6-7).
  o Because the Bible discusses the three kinds of angels with so much detail as to physical form (seraphim having six wings; cherubim having four faces and four wings; four living creatures covered in eyes and each having six wings), it can reasonably be concluded that angels have physical bodies.

i.   If Jesus Died on the Cross, then He was Accursed of God

i.   Dr. Baagil's Argument

Dr. Baagil writes that if Jesus died on the cross, then he was a false prophet and accursed of God according to Deuteronomy:

- "[T]hat prophet or that dreamer of dreams shall be put to death, because he has spoken in order to turn you away from the LORD your God, who brought you out of the land of Egypt and redeemed you from the house of bondage, to entice you from the way in which the LORD your God commanded you to walk. So you shall put away the evil from your midst" (Deu 13:5); and
- "If a man has committed a sin deserving of death, and he is put to death, and you hang him on a tree, his body shall not remain overnight on the tree, but you shall surely bury him that day, so that you do not defile the land which the LORD your God is giving you as an inheritance; for he who is hanged is accursed of God" (Deu 21:22-23).

Therefore, Dr. Baagil believes that Jesus' "death on the cross is to discredit his prophethood. The Jews maintained to have killed Jesus on the cross and consequently portrayed him to be false in his claim to prophethood" (p. 47).

ii.   Problems with Dr. Baagil's Argument

There are several problems with Dr. Baagil's analysis, namely:

(1) Deuteronomy 13:5 Is Referring to False Prophets, Not to Jesus

Deuteronomy 13:5 does not refer to true prophets in the sense of Jesus or other *bona fide* prophets; rather, it is referring to sorcerers, wizards and witches who were to be put to death. Rather, it is referring to false prophets who teach the Jews to "go after other gods" and to "serve them" (Deu 13:2). This verse is therefore irrelevant to Jesus and other *bona fide* prophets who teach the people the true ways of God.

(2) Not All who are Put to Death are False Prophets

It would be wrong to conclude that just because a person was put to death by the Jews, he is automatically to be characterized as a false prophet who is to be put to death. The Old Testament law required the death penalty of many other kinds of offenses, such as adultery (Lev 20:10) and cursing one's parents (Exo 21:17). It would therefore be wrong to conclude that everyone put to death by the Jews was a false prophet engaged in witchcraft and related practices.

(3) There are Some *Bona Fide* Prophets Who are Put to Death by the Jews

There were *bona fide* prophets who were put to death by the Jews. For example, the Jewish people conspired against Zechariah and at King Joash's command, stoned him in the temple court (2Ch 24:21). Similarly, King Jehoiakim intended to put the prophet Uriah to death. After Uriah fled to Egypt (Jer 26:21), King Jehoiakim sent men (Jer 26:22) who returned with Uriah to King Jehoiakim, who put him to death with the sword (Jer 26:23). The fact that Zechariah and Uriah were put to death does not indicate that under Deuteronomy 13:5, they were false prophets who turned the Jews away from God. In fact, it is just the opposite: The Jews were already so far from God that they put to death His holy messengers.

(4) He Who Hangs on a Tree is Accursed of God

Deuteronomy 21:22 discusses the circumstances under which one is to hang "on a tree" and verse 23 states that "he who is hanged is accursed of God" (Deu 21:22-23). Far from undermining the truth of Jesus' crucifixion, it confirms it. Paul writes that those who "are of the works of the law"—*i.e.*, those who refuse God's grace and pursue righteousness through works—are cursed, for "cursed is everyone who does not continue in all things which are written in the book of the law, to do them" (Gal 3:10). No one has fulfilled all things written in the law perfectly, for "all have sinned and fall short of the glory of God" (Rom 3:23). Therefore, all are cursed. Yet by faith, we are justified (Gal 3:11), for "Christ has redeemed us from the curse of the law, having become a curse for us" (Gal 3:13). In writing his letter to Galatians, Paul specifically cites the passage in Deuteronomy 21:22 ("cursed is everyone who hangs on a tree") to demonstrate that while we are all under the curse resulting from violating God's holy law, Christ became that curse in order to set us free. Jesus became a curse "for us" (Gal 3:13), thus satisfying divine justice (Rom 3:26).

j. God Desires Mercy, Not Sacrifice; Therefore, Jesus Did Not Have to Die on the Cross

In his final argument in negating Jesus' crucifixion, Dr. Baagil cites Hosea 6:6: "I desire mercy and not sacrifice, and the knowledge of God more than burnt offerings." Since God does not desire sacrifice, Jesus' death on the cross as a sacrifice for our sins was unnecessary to satisfy God's judgment (p. 47).

Dr. Baagil's error is his misunderstanding of the meta-narrative of Hosea. God does not negate the need for sacrifice to satisfy His perfect justice, which is dealt with thoroughly throughout the rest of the Old Testament, including, for example, in the book of Amos, which focuses to a great extent on God's judgment. Rather, the point that Hosea makes is that sacrifice, or any other conformity to an external ritual, when absent the right inner attitude, is ineffective. Hosea accuses Israel, Ephraim and Judah of engaging in idolatry and of saying to the work of their hands, "you are our gods" (Hos 14:3), while evidently engaging in temple sacrifices and other external practices. Hosea's message is that such rituals are insufficient in keeping God's judgment at bay, for God's desire is for mercy, not sacrifice, and for knowledge of God, not burned offerings (Hos 6:6). External conformity to the letter of the law has no value when right inner attitudes are lacking. It is for this reason that Hosea calls Israel and Judah to repentance (Hos 14:1-9). In other words, the issue is not that sacrifice has no place in God's system of justice, but rather, that sacrifice and conformity to the letter of the law absent conformity to the spirit of the law has no place in satisfying God's justice.

This is precisely why Jesus quoted Hosea 6:6 to self-righteous Pharisees who believed they had God's favor through their external actions, first in Matthew 12:1-7, where the Pharisees accused Jesus' disciples of violating the Sabbath, and then in Matthew 9:10-13, where the Pharisees accused Jesus of eating with tax collectors and sinners. Hosea's words show that God's concerns reach far deeper than external behavior or conformity to the letter of the law. This is why Jesus later characterized the Pharisees as "whitewashed tombs" on the outside, but "full of dead men's bones and all uncleanness" on the inside (Mat 23:27).

God's concern with inner goodness rather than conformity to vain, external ritual is further reinforced in Isaiah's prophecy, where God declares:

Bring no more vain sacrifices; incense is an abomination unto me. The new moon, Sabbath and the calling of assemblies—I cannot endure iniquity and the solemn meeting. My soul hates your new moons and appointed feasts; I am weary of bearing them. When you spread your hands, I will hide my eyes from you; when you pray, I will not hear: your hands are full of blood. Wash yourselves, make yourselves clean; put away the evil of your doings from before my eyes; cease to do evil. Learn to do good; seek justice, relieve the oppressed; defend the fatherless, plead the case of the widow (Isa 1:13-17).

In Isaiah, God is more concerned with "doing good" than in vain sacrifices.

k. It Was Paul Who Taught the Resurrection

Next, Dr. Baagil writes that "[i]t was Paul who taught the resurrection," for Paul "preached to them Jesus and the resurrection" (Acts 17:18) (p. 48). Here, Dr. Baagil's implication is that the resurrection as a teaching was invented by Paul. However, the resurrection was taught and prophesied in the Bible long before Paul even became a disciple.

i. Jesus Prophecies His Resurrection

Jesus also repeatedly prophesied both his death and resurrection throughout the Gospel accounts:

- While they were staying in Galilee, Jesus said to the disciples, "The Son of Man is about to be betrayed into the hands of men, and they will kill Him, and the third day He will be raised up" (Mat 17:22-23).
- Jesus took the twelve disciples aside and began to tell them the things that would happen to Him: "Behold, we are going up to Jerusalem, and the Son of Man will be betrayed to the chief priests and to the scribes; and they will condemn Him to death and deliver Him to the Gentiles; and they will mock Him, and scourge Him, and spit on Him, and kill Him. And the third day He will rise again" (Mark 10:32-34).
- Jesus took the twelve disciples aside and said to them, "Behold, we are going up to Jerusalem, and all things that are written by the prophets concerning the Son of Man will be accomplished. For He will be delivered to the Gentiles and will be mocked

and insulted and spit upon. They will scourge Him and kill Him. And the third day He will rise again" (Luke 18:31-33).

- Moreover, Jesus predicts that he will arise from the "heart of the earth" in a metaphor with Jonah: "As Jonah was three days and three nights in the stomach of the whale, so will the Son of man be three days and three nights in the heart of the earth" (Mat 12:40).

ii. Old Testament Prophecies of the Old Testament

While not as direct as the prophecies spoken by Jesus Himself about His resurrection, the Old Testament also prophesies Jesus' resurrection:

- "Therefore my heart is glad, and my glory rejoices; My flesh also will rest in hope. For You will not leave my soul in Sheol, Nor will You allow Your Holy One to see corruption. You will show me the path of life; In Your presence is fullness of joy; At Your right hand are pleasures forevermore" (Psa 16:9-11). These verses speak first of Jesus' burial, then His descent into Hades, followed by His return into His body resting in the tomb before decay begins, then His resurrection and ascension into heaven to be seated at the Father's "right hand" (Psa 16:11).

- "My God, My God, why have You forsaken Me? Why are You so far from helping Me, and from the words of My crying (Psa 22:1)? I cry in the daytime, but You do not hear; and at night, and am not silent (Psa 22:2). I am poured out like water, and all my bones are disjointed. My heart has turned to wax and has melted. My mouth is dried up and my tongue sticks to the roof of my mouth; you lay me in the dust of death (Psa 22:14-15). All of my bones are on display (Psa 22:17). They divide up and cast lots for my garment (Psa 22:18)." Psalm 22 begins as a prophecy of Jesus' death, but then the shift changes as God looks down at His afflicted servant and answers His cry: "The Lord has not despised the affliction of the afflicted or hidden His face from Him; But gave an answer when He cried to Him (Psa 22:24). I will praise You in the great assembly (Psa 22:25)." The Psalm continuous with a description of a victorious new kingdom: "The poor shall feast (Psa 22:26); those who seek Him will praise the Lord. your heart will live

forever (Psa 22:26). The ends of the world will remember and
turn to the Lord and all the nations will worship You (Psa
22:27). For the Lord rules the nations (Psa 22:28). The
prosperous shall worship; those who go down to the dust will
bow before Him, even he who cannot remain alive (Psa 22:29).
Posterity shall serve Him (Psa 22:30) and come and declare His
righteousness to a people of the future (Psa 22:31)."

- "They made His grave with the wicked-- But with the rich at
His death, Because He had done no violence, Nor was any
deceit in His mouth. Yet it pleased the LORD to bruise Him;
He has put Him to grief. When You make His soul an offering
for sin, He shall see His seed, He shall prolong His days, And
the pleasure of the Lord shall prosper in His hand. He shall see
the labor of His soul, and be satisfied. By His knowledge My
righteous Servant shall justify many, For He shall bear their
iniquities" (Isa 53:9-11). Though Jesus (God's suffering
servant) will be put to and into a "grave (Isa 53:9), He shall
"see His seed" and "prolong His days" (Isa 53:10). This
implies that He will live. Also, "He shall see the labor of His
soul" (Isa 53:11) is rendered as "he will see the light of life" in
the NIV, which references the Dead Sea Scrolls in the
footnotes but notes that the Masoretic Text does not have "the
light of life." If "light of life" was in the original text, it would
further point to Jesus' resurrection after His suffering.

- Hosea writes that "After two days He will revive us; On the
third day He will raise us up, That we may live in His sight"
(Hos 6:2). This prophecy came into fruition when, after Jesus'
resurrection on the third day, bodies were revived and raised up
from the dead: "many bodies of the saints who had fallen
asleep were raised; and coming out of the graves after His
resurrection, they went into the holy city and appeared to
many" (Mat 27:52-53).

D. Specific Topics Relating to "Prophecies" of Muhammad in the Bible

1. The "Chariot of Camels" as Prophecy of Muhammad

a. *Dr. Baagil's Interpretation of Isaiah 21:7 as a Prophecy of the Coming of Muhammad*

The book continues: "Isaiah mentioned this after he saw in a vision a chariot of asses and a chariot of camels (21:7): 'And he saw a chariot with a couple of horsemen, a chariot of asses, and a chariot of camels; and he hearkened diligently with much heed.' The chariot of asses turned out to be Jesus who entered Jerusalem (John 12:14; Matthew 21:5). Who then was the chariot of camels? It could not be other than Muhammad (PBUH) who came about six hundred years after the advent of Messiah" (p. 18).

Dr. Baagil continues this line of reasoning on page 59: "Who, then, is the promised rider on a camel? This powerful Prophet has been overlooked by Bible readers. This is Prophet Muhammad [PBUH]. If this is not applied to him, then the prophecy has yet to be fulfilled. That is why Isaiah mentioned further in the same chapter (21:13): "The burden upon Arabia . . :" which means the responsibility of the Arab Muslims, and of course now of all Muslims, to spread the message of Islam."

b.   Original Hebrew of Isaiah 21:7

The original Hebrew of Isaiah 21:7 states: פרשים רכב חמור רכב גמל:

- פרשים (*pârâsh*, H6571), meaning "horse, steed, warhorse";
- רכב (*rekeb*, H7393), meaning "a team, chariot, chariotry, mill-stone, riders";
- חמור (*chamowr*, H2543), meaning "ass" (donkey);
- רכב (*rekeb*, H7393), as indicated above;
- גמל (*gamal*, H1581), meaning "camel."

The word being used by Dr. Baagil as "chariot" is actually a broader term that can refer to a team, chariot or riders. It is generally translated in the plural in English (*e.g.*, "Elam bore the quiver with chariots of men and horsemen" (Isa 22:6)). The ambiguity of the Hebrew word is the reason for many Isaiah 21:7. Amongst these variations, the NJKV is the only major modern one to render the phrase as a single chariot of asses and a single chariot of camels. Other major translations either render chariots in the plural (*e.g.*, the BBE ("war-carriages with asses, war-carriages with camels")) or otherwise translate it as a reference to riders (plural):

- "riders on donkeys, riders on camels" (ESV);
- "riders on donkeys or riders on camels" (ISV);

- "riders on donkeys or riders on camels" (NIV);
- "riders on asses, riders on camels" (RSV).

Albert Barnes' Notes on the Bible sheds further light on this. He writes:

> The word רכב rekeb denotes properly a chariot or wagon Jdg 5:28; a collection of wagons 2Ch 1:14; 2Ch 8:6; 2Ch 9:25; and sometimes refers to the "horses or men" attached to a chariot. 'David hamstrung all the chariots' 2Sa 8:4; that is, all the "horses" belonging to them. 'David killed of the Syrians seven hundred chariots' 2Sa 10:18; that is, all "the men" belonging to seven hundred chariots. According to the present Masoretic pointing, the word רכב rekeb does not mean, perhaps, anything else than a chariot strictly, but other forms of the word with the same letters denote "riders or cavalry." Thus, the word רכב rakâb denotes a horseman 2Ki 9:17; a charioteer or driver of a chariot 1Ki 22:34; Jer 51:21. The verb רבב râbab means "to ride," and is usually applied to riding on the backs of horses or camels; and the sense here is, that the watchman saw "a riding," or persons riding two abreast; that is, "cavalry," or men borne on horses, and camels, and asses, and hastening to attack the city.

c.   *Problems with Dr. Baagil's Interpretation*

i.   The Plural Use of רכב (rekeb)

Dr. Baagil's interpretation can only work if the first reference to רכב (*rekeb*) in the Hebrew is a single chariot ridden by Jesus or otherwise refers to Jesus as the rider and the second one is a single chariot ridden by Muhammad or otherwise refers to Muhammad as the rider. However, if in fact רכב (*rekeb*) is intended to be read in the plural, as it often is used in Hebrew and as it is rendered in several translations, then Dr. Baagil's reading is flawed. If there are several chariots of asses or one chariot with several riders, then only one of the chariots can be ridden by Jesus and only one of the riders can be Jesus. Who then are the other riders or chariots? The same is true for the plural chariots of camels or the plural riders of a chariot of camels, since there was only one Muhammad.

If in fact the term רכב (*rekeb*) is meant to refer to chariots or riders in the plural, then Dr. Baagil's interpretation is flawed.

ii.   Isaiah 21:7 Does not Refer to Prophets

Yet even if רכב (*rekeb*) is meant to refer to a singular chariot, Dr. Baagil's interpretation still makes no sense in light of the context. Dr. Baagil implies that Isaiah 21:7 is a prophecy of future prophets to come, asking the reader, "Who, then, is the promised rider on a camel?" (p. 59). Yet nothing in Isaiah 21 connotes or denotes that it is speaking of future prophets. Rather, it deals with a prophecy of the fall of Babylon (Isa 21:1, 9). The language is steeped in warfare, with Elam (a perpetual enemy of Babylon) and Media (northwest Iran) commanded to attack (Isa 21:2). Within this context, the chariots (or riders) of asses and camels most likely hold a war function. Per *Albert Barnes' Notes on the Bible*, "[a]sses were formerly used in war where horses could not be procured" and "[c]amels also were used in war, perhaps usually to carry the baggage."

In the present case, the Lord commands Isaiah to post a lookout to report what he sees (Isa 21:6). He is most likely commanding Isaiah to be vigilant on the walls of Jerusalem (where Isaiah was) of oncoming chariots. In Isaiah 21:9, we read that a chariot finally did appear and it contained a messenger bearing the message that Babylon had fallen. The message came to fruition in 689 BC, when Babylon fell, centuries before Jesus or Muhammad appeared.

iii. Dr. Baagil's Loose Logic Leaves Room for Wild Interpretation

Dr. Baagil offers no evidence whatsoever that the chariots referenced in Isaiah 21:7 were prophecies of Jesus and Muhammad, other than the fact that Jesus rode an ass into Jerusalem. No link is established between the chariot of camels and Muhammad, other than the indirect suggestion that both Muhammad and camels were from Arabia. Yet references to "camels" are so frequent in the Bible (more than fifty in the Old Testament alone) that they could be references to any biblical figure by applying Dr. Baagil's loose logic.

If we are to accept Dr. Baagil's speculative interpretation, then what are we to say, for example, of Isaiah 30:6, which references lions, vipers, serpents, donkeys and camels? Are each of these animals a prophecy of some future to come? If so, the reader is left wondering which symbolizes Guru Nanak, which symbolizes Joseph Smith and which symbolizes Bahá'u'lláh.

2. Ishmael was Abraham's Promised Seed and the Son of the Covenant

a. Isaac was not yet Born when Abraham Sent Hagar and Ishmael Away

According to the book of Genesis, as Isaac grew and was weaned (Gen 21:8), Sarah saw Ishmael scoffing at him (Gen 21:9). Therefore, she told Abraham to cast out Hagar and Ishmael (Gen 21:10). God confirmed the matter to Abraham (Gen 21:12-13) and Abraham sent Hagar and Ishmael away, where they wandered in the Wilderness of Beersheba (Gen 21:14).

Dr. Baagil disputes this account and argues that in the biblical account, when Hagar and Ishmael were sent away by Abraham, Ishmael would have been too young for Isaac to have been born. Therefore, Hagar and Ishmael were not cast away: "According to the Islamic version, Abraham took Ishmael and Hagar and made a new settlement in Mecca, called Paean in the Bible (Genesis 21:21), because of a divine instruction given to Abraham as a part of God's plan" (p. 51).

Dr. Baagil supports his argument on the following basis:

- The Bible shows that Ishmael was a teenager when Isaac was born: Abram was 86 years old when Ishmael was born (Gen 16:15-16) and 100 years old when Isaac was born (Gen 21:5). Ishmael was therefore 14 years old when Isaac was born.
- However, when Abraham sent Hagar and Ishmael away, Ishmael was a small child (p. 51), since in the Genesis 21 account, Ishmael is depicted "as a baby put on the shoulder of his mother, called lad and child" (p. 51).
- Thus, when Abraham sent Hagar and Ishmael away, Isaac was not yet born.
- Therefore, Abraham sent Hagar and Ishmael away *not* because Ishmael scoffed at Isaac, since Isaac was not yet born, but rather, for some other reason (Dr. Baagil offers the Islamic explanation of Ishmael and Hagar's establishing a new settlement in Mecca).

Dr. Baagil's argument is problematic for the following reasons:

- With careful reading, one finds that there is indeed no contradiction:
  - Genesis 21:14 does not depict Ishmael "as a baby put on the shoulder of his mother" (p. 51). Rather, it states

that Abraham put the skin of water on Hagar's shoulder: Abraham rose early in the morning, and took bread and a skin of water; and putting it on her shoulder, he gave it and the boy to Hagar, and sent her away" (Gen 21:14). The ASV makes this even clearer in specifying that Abraham "took bread and a bottle of water, and gave it unto Hagar, putting it on her shoulder" (Gen 21:14).

o   In Genesis 21:18, an angel does not instruct Hagar to carry Ishmael, as a baby, in her arms. Rather, the angel instructed Hagar to "lift up the lad and hold him with your hand" (Gen 21:18). Hagar was being instructed to move the boy upward and then hold his hand, for she would soon see a well and give the boy a drink (Gen 21:19). "Lifting up the lad" (Gen 21:18) could have simply been a reference to lifting him out of the shrubs where he was placed (Gen 21:15) and holding him by the hand is a different act from carrying him in her arms.

o   Although Genesis 21 refers to Ishmael as a "lad" and "child," these terms are *not* equivalent to "baby," as Dr. Baagil suggests. A "lad" in the Concise Oxford English Dictionary refers to a "boy" or "young man," not to a baby. The more general term "child" is defined as "a young human being below the age of full physical development" or "a son or daughter of any age." Ishmael at 14 years old could have been referred to as either a "lad" or a "child." In fact, the Bible uses the term "child" to even refer to King Agag of the Amelekites, who was a grown man and yet still a "child" of his mother. Consider, for example, Samuel's words to King Agag just before he cut him into pieces: "As your sword has made women childless, so shall your mother be childless among women" (1Sa 15:33). If Samuel used the term to refer only to babies, then his mother would have been childless even before Samuel put Agag to death, since Agag's mother had no baby children at the time. Rather, it was only in putting Agag, a grown man, to death, that Agag's mother could be said to be "childless." His employment of the term "child" to refer generically to any son or daughter is no different from the use of child in the Genesis 21 account.

- Yet even if Dr. Baagil has identified a genuine biblical contradiction, he shows no support for reading the account of the age of Abraham at Ishmael and Isaac's birth as being more reliable than the account of Hagar and Ishmael's banishment and wandering in the desert. Rather, he creates an artificial contradiction and picks the account that supports his reading of the texts without offering any evidence for the reliability of that reading.

b. *Ishmael, Not Isaac, was the Son of the Covenant*

Dr. Baagil argues that when Genesis 22:2 mentions "your only son Isaac" in instructing Abraham's sacrifice, it must in reality be referring to Ishmael, because at the time Isaac was born, Abraham already had two sons. However, before Isaac was born, Ishmael was his only son. Therefore, "your only son" can only logically refer to Ishmael (p. 53).

There are several problems with this interpretation:

- Dr. Baagil fails to read the rest of Genesis 22:2, which continues, "your only son Isaac, *whom you love*" (emphasis added): Genesis 22:2 is evidently referring to the only son that Isaac loves. In the original Hebrew, this is emphasized in the placement of the reference to "Isaac" *after* the reference to "whom you love": "your only son, whom you love—Isaac."
- Dr. Baagil's argument that "Isaac" in Genesis 22:2 is a substitution of an earlier text in which Ishmael was to be sacrificed makes no sense in light of the biblical text. First, Isaac was already born in the earlier chapter (see Gen 21:2). Therefore, even if the Jews *did* corrupt Genesis 22:2, the text *still* would not make sense if reading "only son" (apart from "only son *whom you love*") as being Ismael, since at the time of the sacrifice, Isaac was also born. Second, Ishmael and Hagar had already been sent away from Abraham in (see Gen 21:9-14) by the time God ordered Abraham to sacrifice his son in Genesis 22:2.

c. *God Would Bless Abraham's Descendants through Ishmael, Not Isaac*

Next, Dr. Baagil argues that God's promise to Abraham in Genesis 22:17 ("blessing I will bless you, and multiplying I will multiply your descendants as the stars of the heaven and as the sand which is on the seashore; and your descendants shall possess the gate of their enemies") would be fulfilled through Ishmael, not Isaac, because it falls within God's earlier promises to multiply Ishmael (p. 53):

- First, in Genesis 17:20: "as for Ishmael, I have heard you. Behold, I have blessed him, and will make him fruitful, and will multiply him exceedingly. He shall beget twelve princes, and I will make him a great nation"; and
- Then, in Genesis 21:18: "lift up the lad and hold him with your hand, for I will make him a great nation" (p. 53).

Dr. Baagil is correct in pointing out that God promised to multiply Ishmael's descendants. However, Dr. Baagil's account is marked by many material omissions. In God's promise to Abraham in Genesis 22:17, he states not only that he will multiply Abraham's descendants (Gen 22:17), but also that Abraham's seed would bless all of the nations of the earth (Gen 22:18). This line can hardly be compared to that promised to Ishmael, who would be a "wild man" whose "hand shall be against every man" (Gen 16:12). In other words, while Isaac's seed would be a blessing to every man (ultimately, in bearing the seed of the savior and messiah Jesus Christ, who would bring salvation to all by grace through faith), Ismael's line would bring conflict and discord (Gen 16:12).

Moreover, Dr. Baagil's mistaken reading of Genesis 22:17 is due to his failure to read the passages surrounding Genesis 17:20:

- Before promising to make Ishmael a great nation in Genesis 17:20, God told Abraham that "Sarah your wife shall bear you a son, and you shall call his name Isaac; I will establish My covenant with him for an everlasting covenant, and with his descendants after him" (Gen 17:19).
- After the promise relating to Ishmael, God also said, "But My covenant I will establish with Isaac" (Gen 17:21).

In other words, both Ishmael and Isaac would have descendants, but God's covenant would be through Isaac's line.

d.   Refuting the Claim that Ishmael was an Illegitimate Son

Dr. Baagil takes the Christian and Jewish claim that "Ishmael was an illegitimate son" (p. 54) and asks, "How could a great Prophet like Abraham have an illegal wife and a son out of wedlock!" (p. 54).

Dr. Baagil's argument is flawed in the following respects:

- Christians do not believe that Ishmael was illegitimate; rather, they acknowledge that Sarai gave her maid Hagar to Abram to be his wife and to conceive children (Gen 16:1-3). Therefore, Ishmael was not conceived in fornication. However, Christians do not believe that Ishmael was the son of the promise, for God told Abraham that God would establish His covenant with Sarah's son (Gen 17:19), Isaac (Gen 17:21).

- While Christians do not believe that Ishmael was illegitimate, they believe that he was conceived in doubt and lack of faith. Abram believed God's promise to give Abram an heir from his own body (Gen 15:4), but rather than wait for God's miracle to take place in its own time, Abram heeded the voice of Sarai (Gen 16:1-3) and conceived through Hagar (Gen 16:4), giving birth to a son of the flesh. Paul writes that "he who was of the bondwoman was born according to the flesh, and he of the freewoman through promise, which things are symbolic. For these are the two covenants: the one from Mount Sinai which gives birth to bondage, which is Hagar—for this Hagar is Mount Sinai in Arabia, and corresponds to Jerusalem which now is, and is in bondage with her children--but the Jerusalem above is free, which is the mother of us all" (Gal 4:23-26). The fact that Paul characterizes Ishmael as having been born according to the flesh, implies that it was not according to God's will.

- That this was not God's will is made evident in the sinful consequences and family brokenness and resentment that resulted. When Hagar saw that she had conceived, Sarai became despised in her eyes (Gen 16:4). Sarai dealt harshly with Hagar and Hagar fled from her presence (Gen 16:6). Hagar was to give birth to a wild man whose hand would be against every man, and every man's hand would be against him (Gen 16:12). Ishmael scoffed at Isaac when he had weaned (Gen 21:9). Sarah took offense at Ishmael's scoffing and sent both him and Hagar away (Gen 21:10). Abraham was saddened by this, as Ishmael was also his son (Gen 21:11). This bitterness and division is not the fruit that comes about when God's will is followed.

- Muslims have difficulty accepting that a prophet could commit sin or act in a way that departs from God's will. However, Abraham was not, strictly speaking, a prophet, at least not in the sense of Elijah, Elisha, Isaiah, Jonah, etc., whose livelihoods were dedicated to the prophetic office. Rather, Abraham was primarily a Patriarch, the father of a nation, and though he received God's revelation, he was never commanded to take this message to the people or to preach. The promises that he would have an heir from his own body (Gen 15:4) and that his descendants would be as numerous as the stars (Gen 15:5) were for his own knowledge, in the same way that the promise to Mary that she would conceive a son by the Holy Spirit (Luke 1:26-39) was for her own knowledge and did not make her into a prophetess.

- Yet even if we were to consider Abraham to be a full-time prophet, this on its own does not put him above sin, for "all have sinned and fallen short of the glory of God" (Rom 3:23), including the prophets. For a further discussion, see "The 'Degrading' of Many 'Prophets' in the Bible," above.

3. Muhammad, Not Jesus, as the Prophet who Brought Peace

a. Jeremiah's Reference to the Peaceful Prophet Does Not Apply to Jesus, Who Did Not Bring Peace

Jeremiah writes that "the prophet who prophesies of peace, when the word of the prophet comes to pass, the prophet will be known as one whom the Lord has truly sent" (Jer 28:9). In other words, a prophet who prophesies peace will only come to be recognized as a true prophet when his word comes to pass. However, Dr. Baagil, interpreting this completely out of context as is his habit, interprets this to be a prophecy of a future prophet who would bring peace. Dr. Baagil argues that this prophet is not Jesus, because in Jesus' own words, He came to "bring a sword rather than peace" (Luke 12:51) (p. 56).

Dr. Baagil's argument is flawed for the following reasons:

i. Jeremiah 28:9 Deals with the Criteria for Distinguishing True Prophets from False Prophets, Not with a Future Prophet to Come

Jeremiah 28:9 has nothing to do with a future prophet. Rather, it is Jeremiah's confrontation of the false prophet Hananiah, who prophesied that God would break the yoke of the king of Babylon (Jer 28:2). Jeremiah replied, saying that from early times, the prophets prophesied war and plague, but the prophet who prophesies peace will only be proved to be a prophet if his prediction comes true (Jer 28:8-9).

ii. Jesus Is the Prince of Peace

Yet even if Jeremiah 28:9 was a prediction of a future prophet that would bring peace, then Jesus should not be ruled out on the basis of his words at Luke 12:51-53. In fact, Jesus is the Prince of Peace (Isa 9:6), who came to bring reconciliation between God and man (2Co 5:18).

iii. Jesus Creates Division between Believers and Unbelievers, Even within the Same Family

The references to division that Jesus makes in Mat 10:34-36 and Luke 12:51-53 should not be read as a contradiction to Jesus' message of peace, but rather, as figurative speech indicating the division and conflict that the Gospel brings between *Christ's followers* and *His enemies*, between *believers* and *unbelievers*, sometimes even within the same family. For example, a son who converts to Christ may become divided against his father, who wishes for him to pursue money, prestige and the things of this world, rather than the eternal things of the Kingdom of God. In this way, Jesus sets "a man against his father, a daughter against her mother, and a daughter-in-law against her mother-in-law" (Mat 10:35-36), in fulfillment of the prophet Malachi ("Daughter rises against her mother, Daughter-in-law against her mother-in-law; a man's enemies are the men of his own household" (Mal 7:6)). That Jesus divides families does not mean that He does not bring peace, but rather, that some choose to continue to live in sin and rebel against family members that turn to God in repentance. Yet among those who turn to God in repentance, Christ establishes peace. He has also come to bring peace between God and those who turn to Him in repentance.

iv. Jesus' References to the "Sword" Should Not be Read Literally

Jesus' reference to the "sword" in Luke 22:36 ("he who has no sword, let him sell his garment and buy one") is not meant to be interpreted literally. It is a figure of speech referencing the *perils that would soon face Jesus' followers*. Reading the reference literally would contradict the testimony of the life of Jesus, who never taught self-defense by the sword. In fact, when Peter cut off the high priest's servant's ear at Jesus' arrest at Gethsemane, Jesus instructed him to put away his sword (John 18:10-11) and He healed the servant's ear (Luke 22:51). Rather, Jesus taught his followers not to resist an evil person, but to turn the other cheek (Mat 5:39).

v. If Jeremiah 28:9 is about a Harbinger of Peace, then Muhammad does Not Qualify

Dr. Baagil's implication is that Jeremiah 28:9 predicts a future prophet who would bring peace and, by ruling out Jesus as this prophet, he implies that Jeremiah prophecies the coming of Muhammad, who would bring Islam, the religion of "peace." As already shown above, Jeremiah 28:9 has nothing to do with the coming of a future prophet. Yet even if Jeremiah 28:9 is a prediction of a future prophet to bring peace and Jesus is not this prophet, then Muhammad hardly qualifies as being a harbinger of "peace." If Jesus said that he brought a "sword," then Muhammad not only brought a sword but used it as well, spreading Islam during his lifetime through religious wars across the Arabian Gulf and Levant and later, through his followers, throughout Anatolia, Central Asia, North Africa and the Iberian Peninsula. The militant nature of Islam is reflected in contemporary Muslim society, where virtually every Muslim-majority country, aside for the oil-rich Arabian Gulf countries and a few other exceptions, is either in a state of civil war, civil armed conflict, armed conflict with neighboring states or domestic instability that has led to an exodus of refugees, all of which cannot be said to stand for or represent "peace."

b. *Islam Means "Peace"*

Dr. Baagil again quotes Jesus' words in Matthew 10:34-36 ("Do not think that I came to bring peace on earth. I did not come to bring peace but a sword. For I have come to 'set a man against his father, a daughter against her mother, and a daughter-in-law against her mother-in-law' and 'a man's enemies will be those of his own household'") as evidence that Jesus did not bring peace. He then implies that Muhammad is the one referenced to by Jesus at Matthew 5:9 ("Blessed are the peacemakers") because "Islam means also Peace" (p. 66).

Dr. Baagil's argument is flawed in the follow ways:

- Islam does not mean "peace" but rather, "submission." The Arabic word for "peace," *salaam* (سلام), shares the same root as "Islam," but has a different meaning.
- Jesus' words in Matthew 5:9 have nothing whatsoever to do with Islam. This is made clearer by continuing to read to the end of the verse, which Dr. Baagil omits. The complete verse states, "Blessed are the peacemakers, For they shall be called sons of God" (Mat 5:9). Islam does not believe that anyone, including Jesus, has the right to be called a "son a God." This is made clear by *Surah* 5:18 ("We are the sons of *Allah* and His beloved ones. Say: Why does He then chastise you for your sins? Nay, you are mortals from among those whom He has created").
- As already discussed above, Jesus came to establish peace. His reference to the "sword" in Luke 22:36 is not meant to be read literally (see "Jesus' References to the "Sword" Should Not be Read Literally," above). That He divides families does not mean that He does not bring peace, but rather, that some choose to continue to live in sin and rebel against family members that turn to God in repentance (see "Jesus Creates Division between Believers and Unbelievers, Even in the Same Family," above).
- ("Jeremiah's Reference to the Peaceful Prophet Does Not Apply to Jesus, Who Did Not Bring Peace"),

4. The Scepter Will Depart from Judah When Shiloh—Muhammad—Comes

a. Overview

Next, Dr. Baagil attempts to explain why the prophetic line, after 2,000 years in the line of Isaac, from Moses to Elijah to Elisha to Isaiah to Jonah to John the Baptist to Jesus, would suddenly switch to Ishmael with one, final prophet—Muhammad. The explanation Dr. Baagil provides is based on Genesis 49:10: "The scepter shall not depart from Judah, Nor a lawgiver from between his feet, Until Shiloh comes; And to Him shall be the obedience of the people."

Dr. Baagil acknowledges that Shiloh is the name of a town. It is an ancient city mentioned several times in the Old Testament. It is located in the modern Khirbet Seilun, south of ancient Tirzah and ten miles north of the Israeli settlement of Beth El in the West Bank. However, for Dr. Baagil, it is not a mere town: "its real meaning is peace, tranquility, rest, *i.e.*, Islam. It could never refer to a town here. If it referred to a person, it could be a corruption of Shaluah (Eluhim), i.e., Messenger (of *Allah*)" (p. 56). In other words, God's plan was to send forward messengers from the line of Isaac, until Shiloh (Islam) would come, at which point the prophetic line would switch to Ishmael.

b.   Flaws in Dr. Baagil's Argument

Dr. Baagil's argument is flawed in the following ways:

i.   The Verses Following Genesis 49:10 Make Clear the Reference to Jesus, Not Muhammad

That Genesis 49:10 is speaking about Christ rather than Muhammad is made clear by the verses following it. Genesis 49:11 states that "He washed his garments in wine, and his clothes in the blood of grapes." This is a reference to the Messiah, whose garments would be stained in crushing grapes, a symbol of working salvation. This is made clear in various later Scriptures, which depict Christ's garments as stained in "wine" or "blood":

(1) Isaiah 63

In Isaiah 63, the Messiah is depicted as bringing salvation, staining his garments by trodding the winepress:

> "Who is this who comes from Edom [meaning "red," and also symbolizing the world that hates God's people], with dyed garments from Bozrah, this One who is glorious in His apparel, Traveling in the greatness of His strength? ... Why is Your apparel red, And your garments like one who treads in the winepress?" (Isa 63:1-2).

The Messiah, who brings salvation, symbolized by the treading of grapes, answers:

"I have trodden the winepress alone, And from the peoples no one was with Me ... Their blood is sprinkled upon My garments, And I have stained all My robes ... the day of vengeance is in My heart, And the year of My redeemed has come ... I looked, but there was no one to help, And I wondered that there was no one to uphold; Therefore My own arm brought salvation for Me" (Isa 63:3-5).

(2) Revelation 19

In Revelation 19, the Apostle John sees the "Word of God" (Jesus), "clothed with a robe dipped in blood, and His name is called The Word of God. And the armies in heaven, clothed in fine linen, white and clean, followed Him on white horses ... He Himself treads the winepress of the fierceness and wrath of Almighty God" (Rev 19:13-15).

(3) Conclusion: Genesis 49:10 must be a Reference to Jesus, the Messiah

Jesus, as Messiah, worked salvation and "washed his garments in wine," per Isaiah 63:2-3 and Revelation 19:13-15. Therefore, the reference to "Shiloh" in Genesis 49, which also references the one who washes his garments in wine (Gen 49:11), is a reference to Jesus. It would not be fitting that these references would point to Muhammad, who neither was a messiah that brought about salvation nor "washed his garments in wine."

ii. The "Scepter" Connotes Judah's Kingship, Not Muhammad's Prophetic Office

Genesis 49:10 refers to a "scepter" that would depart from Judah. A scepter is a ceremonial or emblematic staff that symbolizes royal authority. It is therefore a reference to a ruler, not a prophet. We are therefore to understand Genesis 49:10 as a prophecy of the rulers over Israel, who would come from the line of Judah. This is further made clear by the earlier verses, where Jacob prophecies of Judah: "Judah, you are he whom your brothers shall praise; Your hand shall be on the neck of your enemies; Your father's children shall bow down before you" (Gen 49:8). Clearly, then, Judah's descendants would become kings who would hold a "scepter." This prophecy is later realized God's selection of David as king (1Sa 13:14) and David's anointment by Samuel (1Sa 16:11-13). Therefore, Genesis 49:10 states that the ruling line will not depart from Judah.

That the scepter would be passed on to Muhammad makes no sense in light of the context of Genesis 49:10 because Muhammad was never a king. Jesus, in contrast, was "king of kings" (1Ti 6:15).

iii. If "Shiloh" Means Peace, Then It Refers to Jesus, Not Muhammad

If "Shiloh" means peace, then it cannot be Muhammad, because Muhammad did not bring peace. As discussed above, Muhammad spread Islam during his lifetime through religious wars across the Arabian Gulf and Levant and later, through his followers, throughout Anatolia, Central Asia, North Africa and the Iberian Peninsula. The militant nature of Islam is reflected in contemporary Muslim society, where virtually every Muslim-majority country, aside for the oil-rich Arabian Gulf countries and a few other exceptions, is either in a state of civil war, civil armed conflict, armed conflict with neighboring states or domestic instability that has led to an exodus of refugees, all of which cannot be said to stand for or represent "peace."

iv. "Until" Does Not Connote that the Scepter will ever be Transferred from Judah

It may be easy to misinterpret Genesis 49:10 to mean that the scepter *will* depart from Judah when Shiloh comes, since it states that it will *not* depart "until" Shiloh comes (Gen 49:10). However, one must have a clear understanding of the use of the word "until" in the Bible before drawing such a conclusion.

The Hebrew word עַד (*ad*, H5704), which is often translated into English as "till" or "until," should be understood to have a broader meaning. The Hebrew עַד is used, for example, in Genesis 8:5: "the waters decreased continually until the tenth month. In the tenth month, on the first day of the month, the tops of the mountains were seen." If the word "until" means that the condition stated before "until" did not continue thereafter, then the flood waters would have remained to the mountaintops even thereafter. Of course, the waters continued to decrease even after the tenth month.

The same Hebrew word עַד, if is used in 2 Samuel to connote a change in a condition after a fact specified, would lead to illogical results. The text states that "Michal, Saul's daughter, had no child till the day of her death" (2Sa 6:23) (BBE). If "till" (עַד) is taken to mean that the thing that did not happen before Michal's death (her bearing of children) necessarily happened thereafter, then Michal must have had children after her death. With this illogical conclusion, we must conclude that the proper understanding of the Hebrew עַד both here and elsewhere, including in Genesis 49:10, connotes the meaning "before" alongside "until."

The Greek word rendered as "till" or "until" in English (ἕως (he'-ōs, G2193)) also has a broader meaning than its English rendition and can also be translated as "while" or even "before," but that is not particularly relevant for the present Hebrew word study.

The point to remember is that the scepter would remain with Judah in all of the years preceding (until) the coming of Shiloh (Jesus). At that point, Genesis 49:10 does not explicitly state what will happen with the scepter. It does not necessarily mean that it would be transferred to another after Shiloh comes.

5. Baca as Mecca

a. *Christian View of the Valley of Baca*

The Valley of Baca is referenced in Psalm 84:4-6:

> Blessed are those who dwell in Your house; They will still be praising You. Selah. Blessed is the man whose strength is in You, Whose heart is set on pilgrimage. As they pass through the Valley of Baca, They make it a spring; The rain also covers it with pools.

According to the NIV Study Bible, *Baca* means either "weeping" or "balsam trees" common in arid valleys. "The place is unknown and may be figurative (see 23:4) for arid stretches the pilgrims had to traverse" (p. 875).

b. *Ghada Khafagy's Argument*

i.   Overview

While Ghada Khafagy does not explicitly state that Psalm 84:4-6 refers to pilgrimage to Mecca rather than to Jerusalem, she certainly implies it. She writes that "we read in the Bible (Psalms 84:4-6) words referring to pilgrims who praise God in the Valley of Baca,"[2] and then

---

[2]   Available   at
<http://ascertainthetruth.com/att/index.php?option=com_content&view=article&id=377:where-hearts-a-souls-meet&catid=64:understanding-al-islam&Itemid=53>.

quotes Psalms 84:4-6, referring to pilgrims passing through the valley of Baca.

ii. Response

Ghada Khafagy's argument is flawed in two ways:

- First, she misstates the Christian Scriptures, which do not state that pilgrims "praise God in the Valley of Baca." Rather, it is "those who dwell in Your house" who praise God (Psa 84:4) and those whose "heart is set on pilgrimage" (Psa 84:5) who "pass through the Valley of Baca" (Psa 84:5). It does not state that the pilgrims necessary praise God while in the Valley of Baca; it simply states that those who dwell in God's house praise him and pilgrims pass through Baca.
- Ms. Khafagy stops quoting the verses at Psalm 84:6. However, if she continued to Psalm 84:7, we would see the full context of the pilgrimage, properly placed in Zion (Jerusalem).

c. *Dr. Baagil's Argument*

Dr. Baagil writes that Mecca is mentioned twice in the *Qur'an*, first as "Mecca" in *Surah* 48:24, then as "Bakka" in *Surah* 3:96 ("Verily, the first House [of worship] appointed for mankind was that in Bakka, full of blessing, and guidance for all people"). He points out that the word "Baca," which appears in some translations of the Old Testament at Psalm 84:6, is the same "Bakka" that appears in *Surah* 3:96 and that, therefore, the author's reference to pilgrimage at Baca proves that prior to the corruption of the Scriptures, the Jews used to make pilgrimage (*hajj*) to Mecca (p. 57).

d. *Christian Response*

Even if Baca is Mecca, as Ghada Khafagy suggests, the verse does not affirm Mecca as the place to which pilgrimage should be performed. The verse, in its full context, reads as follows (Psa 84:4-7):

> Blessed are those who dwell in Your house; They will still be praising You. Selah.
> Blessed is the man whose strength is in You, Whose heart is set on pilgrimage.
> As they pass through the Valley of Baca, They make it a spring; The rain also covers it with pools.

They go from strength to strength; Each one appears before God in Zion.

The NIV translates verse 7 as *"till* each appears before God in Zion" (emphasis added). Zion, of course, is used in the Bible as a synonym of Jerusalem, not Mecca. The scriptures thus discuss a pilgrimage *through* a dry, arid place (Baca) until reaching God in Zion—Jerusalem, the City of David.

i.

Dr. Baagil's argument is flawed in the following respects:

- Psalm 84:5 does not reference "pilgrimage" in the original Hebrew. Rather, it is literally rendered as those "in whose hearts are (the) highways" (probably the highways the Israelites took to observe the religious festivals at Zion (Jerusalem), referenced in 84:7).[3] Some translations (the NIV, NKJV) have rendered the English as "pilgrimage," but even in these translations, the sense is largely figurative (*e.g.*, setting their "hearts on pilgrimage" in the NIV; whose "heart is set on pilgrimage" in the NKJV). This is different from Islamic *hajj*, where the pilgrim literallly physically journeys to Mecca.
- The original Hebrew uses the term בכא (*bâkâ'*, H1056) in Psalm 84:7, which literally means "weeping." The "Valley of Baca" may therefore be a figurative reference to a place of weeping that contrasts the "place of springs" later referenced (Psa 84:6) as the pilgrims move toward Zion.
- If Baca is an actual place and the pilgrimage (or "highways") referenced in 84:5 is literal, then it is highly unlikely that Baca would be Mecca because Mecca, in Islam, is a pilgrimage *destination*, but in the Psalms, the pilgrims "pass through the Valley of Baca" (Psa 84:6) on their way to Zion (Jerusalem) (Psa 84:7). Therefore, why would Jewish pilgrims who were living in the united kingdom of Israel under David's reign when he wrote the Psalms, pass through Mecca on their way to Zion? That would be an unnecessary and inefficient detour. Even if we ignore the evidence showing that the pilgrims were headed towards Zion and conclude that the Jews were going to

---

[3] *See NIV Study Bible* note at p. 875.

Mecca, why would they "pass" (Psa 84:6) through "Baca" (Mecca) on their way to Mecca? Wouldn't they rejoice when they reached Baca, their final destination, rather than continue onward?

- The "spring" referenced in Psalm 84:6 ("As they pass through the Valley of Baca, They make it a spring") is meant to be interpreted figuratively as the joyful expectation of the pilgrims transforming the difficult ways into places of refreshment. Yet Dr. Baagil interprets it literally to mean the *Zamzam* well, which is "close to Ka'bah" (p. 57). For Dr. Baagil, then, the pilgrims pass through Mecca (Baca) in their pilgrimage, making it a "spring," yet the *Zamzam* well is located in Mecca itself, 20 miles east of the *Ka'ba*. Therefore, it would not make sense that they would pass the spring on their way to the Mecca pilgrimage if the spring is located in Mecca itself.

- That the pilgrims are on their way to Mecca is very difficult in light of the context of Psalm 84, which makes specific reference to Jewish practices that do not correspond to Islam. For example, Psalm 84:3 references God's "altars," but Islam does not make use of altars. In Judaism, in contrast, the altar is used for sacrifice from the time of Noah (Gen 8:20). The "tabernacle" (NKJV) or "dwelling place" (NIV) referenced in Psalm 84:1 is the Jewish place of worship, whose frame and structure was commanded of the Israelites by God in Exodus 26. It is made with curtains (Exo 26:1) and is distinct from the black granite *Ka'ba* structure. Also, the "tabernacle" or "dwelling place" (in the translations of Psa 84:1 in, *e.g.*, the ESV and NIV) has the meaning of God's dwelling (consider Solomon's words in 1 Kings 8:27: "will God really dwell on earth? The heavens, even the highest heaven, cannot contain you. How much less this temple I have built!," which captures at least the figurative aspect of God's "dwelling" in the tabernacle). In Islam, in contrast, the *Ka'ba* is considered by some to be the dwelling place of *Allah*, but the Ka'ba's architectural distinctness from the tabernacle make it difficult to argue that the reference to the tabernacle in Psalm 84:1 was in fact referring to *Ka'ba*.

6. Muhammad as the Prophet Like unto Moses

a. *Dr. Baagil's Argument*

Dr. Baagil draws on the Deuteronomy 18:18, "I will raise up for them a Prophet like you from among their brethren, and will put My words in His mouth, and He shall speak to them all that I command Him," which is addressed to Moses, and argues that based on the similarities between Muhammad and Moses, Muhammad is the promised prophet.

Dr. Baagil's argument has the following problems:

b. Flaws in Dr. Baagil's Argument

i.   The Prophet Like Moses was to Come from Among the Israelites, not the Ishmaelites

Deuteronomy 18:18 states that God would raise up a prophet from among the Israelites' brethren. The Hebrew word used for "brother "in Deuteronomy 18:18 is אָח (*'ach*, H251), which generally relates to kinship within the same tribe. It is generally used throughout the Scripture to refer to either a brother of the same parents, a cousin or, in some cases, some other distant but related person. It also has a figurative meaning of resemblance, but the general use of the word to refer to a "kinsman" would indicate that more likely than not, Moses was referring to a fellow-Israeli (*i.e.*, a prophet from among one of the twelve tribes of Israel). However, Dr. Baagil's application of Deuteronomy 18:18 to Muhammad means that it was referring not to a fellow Israeli "brother," but rather, to a completely different line that had previously separated not only from Israel (Jacob), but also from Israel's father Isaac—a descendant of Ishmael. This is unlikely in light of the use of the word "brother" in Deuteronomy 18:18.

If Deuteronomy 18:18 really were simply referring to some relative, then there is no limit as to how creative we can get with the possible candidate. Even a descendant of Isaac's brother Midian could be claimed to be the "prophet" like Moses. Taken to an extreme, any living person can be the prophet since, in an abstractly figurative sense, we are all Israel's "brothers" since we all share the same ancestor Noah, as well as of course Adam.

ii. The Prophet Like Moses is a Reference to a Line of Prophets

The context of Deuteronomy 18:18 makes it clear that Moses was speaking not of Muhammad, but rather, a line of prophets who would later take Moses' place. For example, verses 20-22 speak about how to determine when a prophet's message is genuinely from God.

iii. The Similarities between Moses and Muhammad Are Limited

Dr. Baagil supports his argument that Muhammad is the promised prophet by showing that Moses and Muhammad had many similarities. Namely, he shows that they both: (i) had normal births; (ii) were married with children; (iii) had normal deaths; (iv) were prophets and statesmen; (v) had forced emigrations; (vi) were pursued by their enemies; (vii) had moral and physical victories over their enemies; (viii) had their revelations written down during their lifetimes; (ix) had spiritual and legal teachings; and (x) were initially rejected and then accepted by their people.

(1) Similarities are Randomly Chosen and Limited

The first problem is that Dr. Baagil's similarities are randomly chosen and limited. One can find similar and even more similarities between Moses and many other prophets of the Bible and argue that such prophets are the fulfillment of Deuteronomy 18:18. For example, one can argue that Elisha is the prophet "like Moses" since both he and Moses:

- (i) both had normal births;
- (ii) both were prophets;
- (iii) both had forced emigrations (Jezebel's persecution of Elijah sent him as far as Horeb (1Ki 19:2-8));
- (iv) both were pursued by their enemies (Ahad had searched for and hunted Elijah (1Ki 18:10));
- (v) both had moral and physical victories over their enemies (after Elijah proved that Baal was a false god, he then executed the prophets of Baal (1Ki 18:23-40);
- (vi) both had their revelations written down during their lifetimes. We know this is the case for Elijah because his prophecies made it into the books of the Kings, which were commissioned by the kings to collect together information which had been previously chronicled. Also, Elijah lived at the time of the School of the Prophecy, so the prophetic office was already established and prophets had scribes. Elijah's scribe was probably his servant referenced in 1 Kings 18:43;
- (vii) both had spiritual teachings;

- (viii) both were rejected by the ruler (Moses was rejected by Pharaoh and Elijah was rejected and hunted by King Ahab (*see, e.g.,* 1Ki 18:7-10));
- (ix) both parted waters such that they could cross over on dry land. Moses parted the Red Sea and Elijah parted the Jordan River (2Ki 2:7-9);
- (x) both performed great wonders and miracles. Moses commanded the ten plagues; Elijah caused a widow's bin of flour and jar of oil to multiply (1Ki 17:12 et. seq.) and performed many other great miracles;
- (xi) both were able to control the elements. Moses made hail appear (Exo 9:23) and Elijah caused rain and drought through his prayer (*see* Jas 5:17).
- (xii) both caused fire to come to the ground. Moses sent fire mixed with hail (Exo 9:23) and Elijah called down fire to consume a captain and his fifty men (2Ki 1:10).

Here, we have enumerated 12 similarities. We can find many more, such as both Moses and Elijah being sons of Israel (Jacob). Moreover, there may be other similarities that we cannot directly attest to, since the Bible is silent on some questions. For example, Elijah, like Moses, may have been married with children.

Therefore, if we are to conclude that Muhammad is the prophet prophesied of in Deuteronomy 18:18 because of his similarities to Moses, then we must recognize that there are many other better-qualified prophets who have similarities with Moses than does Muhammad.

(2) There are Substantial *Differences* between Moses and Muhammad

Dr. Baagil suggests that Muhammad is the prophet referenced in Deuteronomy 18:18 on the basis of ten elements that he finds in common between them. Yet he does not cite the substantial differences between them. The following examples are taken from the site *Answering Islam*[4]:

---

[4] See www.answering-islam.org/authors/cornelius/like_moses.html (last accessed 8 Nov. 2013).

- Unlike Moses, Muhammad performed no miraculous signs ("Why are not (signs) sent to him, like those which were sent to Moses?" (Surah 28:48));
- Unlike Moses, who spoke directly with God ("to Moses *Allah* spoke directly" (Surah 4:164)), Muhammad did not ("it is not fitting for a man that *Allah* should speak to him except by inspiration, or from behind a veil, or by the sending of a messenger" (Surah 42:51). The Hadith also makes clear that Muhammad never saw *Allah* ("Whoever claimed that (the Prophet) Muhammad saw his Lord, is committing a great fault, for he only saw Gabriel" (Sahih al-Bukhari, Volume 4, Book 54, No. 457)).
- Unlike Moses, who never thought he was demon-possessed, Muhammad at one point did. In Ibn Ishaq's *Sirat Rasul Allah*, translated by A. Guillaume as *The Life of Muhammad*, Muhammad states that "none of God's creatures was more hateful to me than an (ecstatic) poet or a man possessed: I could not even look at them. I thought, Woe is me poet or possessed — Never shall the Quraysh say this of me! I will go to the top of the mountain and throw myself down that I may kill myself and gain rest" (p. 106).
- Moses remained clear-minded, but Muhammad became mentally confused. As narrated by Aisha in *Sahih al-Bukhari*, "During his sickness, *Allah*'s Apostle was asking repeatedly, "Where am I today? Where will I be tomorrow?" (Volume 2, Book 23, Number 471).
- Moses was never bewitched, but Muhammad was. In *Al-Bukhari*, as Narrated by Aisha "A man called Labid bin al-A'sam from the tribe of Bani Zaraiq worked magic on *Allah*'s Apostle until *Allah*'s Apostle started imagining that he had done a thing that he had not really done. One day or one night he was with us, he invoked *Allah* and invoked for a long period, and then said, 'O Aisha! Do you know that *Allah* has instructed me concerning the matter I have asked him about? Two men came to me and one of them sat near my head and the other replied, 'He is under the effect of magic.' The first one asked, 'Who has worked the magic on him?' The other replied, 'Labid bin Al-Asam'" (Vol. VII, no. 658).
- Muhammad said he was different from all other prophets (including of course Moses). In *Bukhari*, as narrated by Jabir

bin 'Abdullah, Muhammad said, "I have been given five things which were not given to anyone else before me. 1. *Allah* made me victorious by awe (by His frightening my enemies) for a distance of one month's journey. 2. The earth has been made for me (and for my followers) a place for praying and a thing to perform Tayammum, therefore anyone of my followers can pray wherever the time of a prayer is due. 3. The booty has been made Halal (lawful) for me yet it was not lawful for anyone else before me. 4. I have been given the right of intercession (on the Day of Resurrection). 5. Every Prophet used to be sent to his nation only but I have been sent to all mankind" (Volume 1, Book 7, Number 331).

- Moses never replaced his earlier revelations with later ones, but Muhammad did. Surah 2:106 (Pickthall) "Nothing of our revelation (even a single verse) do we abrogate or cause be forgotten, but we bring (in place) one better or the like thereof. Knowest thou not that *Allah* is Able to do all things?"

(3) Muhammad Is Not the Deuteronomy 18:18 Prophet Because He Spoke Word in God's Name Not Commanded of Him

Deuteronomy 18:20 states that "the prophet who presumes to speak a word in My name, which I have not commanded him to speak, or who speaks in the name of other gods" is not a true prophet and thus "shall die."

Muhammad was fooled into uttering Satanic verses. According to the *History of Tabari* (1192-1193) (W. Montgomery Watt, M. V. McDonald, trans.), "That evening Gabriel came to him and reviewed the surah with him, and when he reached the two phrases which Satan had cast upon his tongue he said, 'I did not bring you these two.' Then the Messenger of God said, 'I have fabricated things against God and have imputed to Him words which He has not spoken.' Then God revealed to him: 'And they indeed strove hard to beguile you away from what we have revealed to you, that you should invent other than it against us...' (Surah 17:73)" (Vol. 6, p. 111).

By "fabricat[ing] things against God and ... imput[ing] to Him words which He has not spoken," Muhammad spoke words in God's name that God did not command him to speak, thus contravening Deuteronomy 18:20. Muhammad therefore cannot be the "prophet like Moses" referenced in Deuteronomy 18:18 because Moses never committed any such act.

7. Isaiah 42 as Prophecy of Muhammad's Coming

Next, Dr. Baagil points to Isaiah 42 as a "clearer fulfillment of the prophecy of Muhammad" (p. 62). Dr. Baagil divides his argument into several sections. Those sections that contain a substantial argument (as opposed just a verse citation without any argumentation) are each responded to in turn below.

a. God's Servant

Dr. Baagil first points to Isaiah 42:1 "Behold! My Servant whom I uphold, My Elect One in whom My soul delights! I have put My Spirit upon Him; He will bring forth justice to the Gentiles" and argues that this is a prophecy of the coming of Muhammad. This is problematic for the following reasons:

- If Dr. Baagil wishes to argue that Muhammad is the personification of the Isaiah 42:1 prophet because he is called God's "servant," then every prophet since the time of Moses can similarly be said to be the Isaiah 42:1 personification, since they all served God by speaking His Word.
- Yet of all of these servants, Jesus was the greatest of all; He not only served God, but also served man by giving the ultimate sacrifice, his life (John 3:16). Jesus says, "Greater love has no one than this, than to lay down one's life for his friends" (John 15:13). There is no record of Muhammad making such sacrifice or service.
- Jesus says that the "he who is greatest among you, let him be as the younger, and he who governs as he who serves" and that "I am among you as the One who serves" (Luke 22:27).

b. Will not Cry or Lift His Voice

Isaiah 42:2 continues, "He will not cry out, nor raise His voice, Nor cause His voice to be heard in the street." Dr. Baagil argues that this is a reference to Prophet Muhammad's "decency" (p. 62), but this argument is flawed:

- Isaiah 42:2 does not state anything about decency. Rather, it is about lifting one's voice. If it were about decency, then one would have a difficult case arguing that it foretells Muhammad, who taught his followers to "war on the unbelievers" (*Surah*

9:73) and "Fight unbelievers" (*Surah* 9:123) and who "cut off the hands and feet of the men belonging to the tribe of Uraina and did not cauterize (their bleeding limbs) till they died" (*Sahih al-Bukhari*, Vol 8, Bk 82, Hadith 792) and prescribed retaliation (*Surah* 2:178). Jesus, in contrast, taught his followers "not to resist an evil person" and to "turn the other cheek" (Mat 5:39) and to "love your enemies" and "do good to those who hate you" (Mat 5:44). These teachings are far more decent and merciful than the vengeance-based system taught by Muhammad.

- In reality, Isaiah 42:2 refers not to decency, but rather, to lifting up one's voice. That this is a reference to Jesus is made clear by Matthew, who writes that after healing the multitudes (Mat 12:15), Jesus warned them not to make him known (Mat 12:16) in order to fulfill the words of Isaiah (Matt 12:18-21).
- That Jesus would not quarrel or cry out is a reference to his willing self-sacrifice. Isaiah 53:7 accounts for this in stating, "He was oppressed and He was afflicted, Yet He opened not His mouth; He was led as a lamb to the slaughter, and as a sheep before its shearers is silent, So He opened not His mouth." Of course, this is not a reference to Muhammad. Even Muslims acknowledge that Muhammad was not sacrificed "as a lamb to the slaughter"; rather, he died of natural causes involving illness and fever (*An Introduction to the Quran II*, 1895, p.279).

c. *Will not Fail or Be Discouraged*

Citing Isaiah 42:4 ("He will not fail nor be discouraged"), Dr. Baagil argues that this cannot be a reference to Jesus, "who did not prevail over his enemies and was disappointed because of the rejection by the Israelites" (p. 62). However, Dr. Baagil ignores the Gospel account in its entirety, which proves that Jesus in the end vanquished death and His enemies:

- While it is true that Jesus was crucified, he ultimately prevailed over his enemies by rising from the dead (Mark 16:6).
- Moreover, while the Israelites did initially reject Jesus, many were later converted to Christianity. The greatest examples of these is of course Paul, who in his address to King Agrippa sets forth how he was initially a zealous persecutor of the Christians

and then later dramatically converted to Christianity (Acts 26:1-29). Later, we read of hundreds of other Jews who also converted to Christianity. For example, the Christian elders reported to Paul "how many myriads of Jews there are who have believed" (Acts 21:20).

-   If it is true that Jesus cannot be the Isaiah 42 servant because he was rejected by some Jews, then certainly Muhammad cannot be this figure either because he too was rejected by Jews, both initially and by Jews who to this day do not accept him as a prophet.

d. God will Give the Servant as a "Covenant"

Next, Dr. Baagil points to Isaiah 42:6 ("I, the LORD, have called You in righteousness, and will hold Your hand; I will keep You and give You as a covenant to the people, As a light to the Gentiles") as an indication that Muhammad is the promised prophet. Dr. Baagil interprets this to mean that "no other Prophet will come after him. In a short time many Gentiles were guided into Islam" (p. 63).

This is flawed for the following reasons:

-   First, nothing in the verse cited states that "no other Prophet will come after him," as Baagil suggests. Yet even if this were meant, then the reference would not be to Muhammad, since many have come after him who have received the gift of prophecy, which is given freely as a gift of the Holy Spirit (1Co 12:10), even to this day. Rather, if the verse were referring to the last of the prophets of the law, before through God's grace in Jesus the law was fulfilled, then the last prophet would, according to Christ's words, be John the Baptist (Mat 11:13). Muhammad invented a new legal system that was neither based in the codified law of justice given through Moses nor in the law of grace given by Jesus.

-   Isaiah 42:6 references a "covenant" to the people, which was foreshadowed by Jeremiah, who wrote of "a new covenant" (Jer 31:31). This new covenant, was fulfilled not in Muhammad, but in Jesus, who at the last supper, "took the cup ... saying, 'This cup is the new covenant in My blood, which is shed for you" (Luke 22:20). Jesus' "blood of the new covenant" was "shed for many for the remission of sins" (Mat

26:28). The new covenant that was established replaced the covenant of law with Christ's covenant of grace, through faith.

- Dr. Baagil argues that Isaiah 42:6 refers to Muhammad because it states that the promised prophet will be a "light of the gentiles" and, through Muhammad, "many gentiles were guided into Islam" (p. 63). However, it must be acknowledged that most gentiles were not "guided" into Islam but converted with the sword. Yet even if they were "guided" to Islam, the same could be said about Christianity, which gained myriads of converts from the first century, beginning first with the centurion Cornelius (Acts 10:1) and all of the Gentiles who heard Peter preaching, who received the Holy Spirit (Acts 10:44-46), to the present day, representing over two billion people, effectively making it the world's largest religion.

e.   The Servant will Open Blind eyes and Free Prisoners

Dr. Baagil then quotes Isaiah 42:7: The servant will "open blind eyes, … bring out prisoners from the prison, Those who sit in darkness from the prison house." Dr. Baagil interprets this as a prophecy of Muhammad: "'Blind eyes, life of darkness' denotes here the pagan life. 'Bring out the prisoners from the prison' denotes the abolishment of slavery for the first time in the history of mankind" (p. 63).

Dr. Baagil's interpretation is flawed in the following ways:

i.   "Open Blind Eyes" is a Reference to Jesus

If "open blind eyes" means converting pagans, then Jesus, who was responsible for the conversion of myriads of Roman gentiles to the worship of the one true God (see, *e.g.*, Acts 10), lays just as strong a claim to it as does Muhammad. However, if the reference is interpreted literally, then it can only apply to Jesus, who repeatedly made the blind see (*e.g.*, John 9:1-7, Mat 9:27-30), not to Muhammad.

ii.   "Freeing Prisoners" is a Reference to Jesus

Dr. Baagil believes that the Isaiah 42:7 reference to freeing prisoners refers to the abolishment of slavery. First off, it does not refer to the abolition of slavery. Rather it is a reference to freedom from the figurative "prison" of Babylon and also from spiritual and moral bondage. Throughout the book of Isaiah, the recurrent references to the Lord's promised Servant who was to come to free prisoners point back to Jesus. For example, Isaiah writes, "The Spirit of the Lord God is upon Me, Because the Lord has anointed Me To preach good tidings to the poor; He has sent Me to heal the brokenhearted, To proclaim liberty to the captives, And the opening of the prison to those who are bound" (Isa 61:1). Jesus himself proclaimed that he fulfilled these words (Luke 4:18-21). Jesus led captives free from spiritual and moral bondage by casting out demons (*e.g.*, the boy thrown to the ground convulsing at Luke 9:37-45) and pointing out the way to redemption, causing salvation to come to a tax collector's house (Luke 19:5-9) and causing a woman to turn away from adultery (John 8:3-11).

Ultimately, what Jesus did was set people free from the prison of sin. He said, "you shall know the truth, and the truth shall make you free ... Most assuredly, I say to you, whoever commits sin is a slave of sin. And a slave does not abide in the house forever, but a son abides forever. Therefore if the Son makes you free, you shall be free indeed" (John 8:32-36). Jesus is the "Son" who sets you free.

iii. If "Freeing Prisoners" Refers to Abolition, then It Still Cannot Be a Reference to Muhammad

Even if Isaiah 42:7 referred to the abolishment of slavery, Dr. Baagil's implication that Muhammad brought about "the abolishment of slavery for the first time in the history of mankind" (p. 63) is false. First, slavery was abolished in some places far before Muhammad even appeared on the earth. In 221-206 BC, the Qin Dynasty abolished slavery and established a free peasantry who owed taxes and labor to the state (*The Earth and Its Peoples: A Global History* (Cengage Learning, 2009), p. 165). Slavery was later reinstituted, but after Wang Mang usurped the Chinese throne, slavery was again abolished (*Encyclopedia of Antislavery and Abolition* (Greenwood Publishing Group, 2011), p. 155).

Second, there is no reference to Muhammad having abolished slavery. In reality, slavery continued in Muslim countries far after it had been abolished in western nations. Most Muslim countries only abolished slavery in the twentieth century: Qatar in 1952; 1958: Niger in 1960 (though it was not made illegal until 2003); Yemen in 1962; the United Arab Emirates in 1963; Oman in 1970; Mauritania in 1981; etc. Saudi Arabia, the land where Muhammad prophet taught and received the Qur'an, only abolished slavery in 1962, just little over fifty years ago. And while some Muslim countries have officially abolished slavery, contemporary slavery still exists in many Muslim countries, such as Niger, Mali, Pakistan, the Sudan and Mauritania. Much of the condition of slavery in these countries is documented by reputable agencies and news sources (*see, e.g.*, CNN's "Slavery's last stronghold" special[5]).

f. God's "Glory" Is Muhammad

Next, Dr. Baagil writes that Isaiah 42:8 ("I am the LORD, that is My name; And My glory I will not give to another, Nor My praise to carved images") is a reference to Muhammad, who is "unique among all Prophets as he is the 'Seal of all Prophets' and his teachings remain undistorted until today, compared with Christianity and Judaism" (p. 63).

Dr. Baagil's argument is flawed for the following reasons:

- The very fact that Muhammad is even a prophet has never been established or proven by Dr. Baagil; he is using a conclusion lacking any support or evidence to prove another conclusion similarly lacking support or evidence.
- As already discussed extensively above, Christianity and Judaism have *not* been corrupted. Rather, what is corrupt is Dr. Baagil's twisting of the Scriptures to prove his interpretations of the Christian and Hebrew Scriptures. Yet Dr. Baagil's arguments are filled with contradictions, false statements and errors of logic and his scriptural interpretations are obtuse.
- Yet even if the Bible were corrupt, Isaiah 42:8 says nothing whatsoever about this topic. Rather, it is referring to God's glory, which will be given to His servant. Ultimately, the glory of God is given to Jesus Christ, as testified by John 1:14 ("the Word became flesh and dwelt among us, and we beheld His glory"); John 11:4 (Jesus said, "This sickness is not unto death, but for the glory of God, that the Son of God may be glorified through it"); John 17:4 (Jesus "glorified [God] on the earth"); and Heb 1:3 (Jesus is "the brightness of [God's] glory and the express image of His person").

---

[5]   Available   at
<http://edition.cnn.com/interactive/2012/03/world/mauritania.slaverys.last.stronghol d/index.html>.

g.   The "New Song" to be Sung would be in Arabic

Dr. Baagil writes that Isaiah 42:10 ("Sing to the Lord a new song, and His praise from the ends of the earth") is a reference to Muhammad because the "new song ... is not in Hebrew or Aramaic, but in Arabic" (p. 63). Dr. Baagil's argument is flawed for the following reasons:

- First, he gives no textual support for his interpretation of the Scripture as prophesying a song to be sung in Arabic. Using his loose logic, an adherent of the Bahá'i faith could just as easily read the verse to be a prophecy of the coming of Bahá'u'lláh, who would sing a "new song" not in Hebrew or in Aramaic, but in Persian.
- Second, even if the verse meant that it was the language of the song, rather than the song itself, that would be new, then what is to exclude Jesus, who would "sing a song" in Aramaic rather than in Hebrew? Dr. Baagil rules out the possibility of an Aramaic-speaking prophet not because Isaiah 42:10 rules it out, but because such a possibility undermines the possibility that Isaiah 42 prophesies Muhammad.
- Third, Dr. Baagil has completely misunderstood the meaning of Isaiah 42:10. The "new song" that will be sung is about the Isaiah 42:9 "new things" that Isaiah declares. These "new things" are the liberation from Babylon and restoration of Israel.

h.   Isaiah 42 Cannot be Applied to an Israelite Prophet because Kedar is a Son of Ishmael

Isaiah 42 states: "Let the wilderness and its cities lift up their voice, The villages that Kedar inhabits. Let the inhabitants of Sela sing, Let them shout from the top of the mountains. Let them give glory to the Lord, And declare His praise in the coastlands" (42:11-12).

Dr. Baagil points to Isaiah 42:11 ("Let the wilderness and its cities lift up their voice, the villages that Kedar inhabits. Let the inhabitants of Sela sing") as evidence that Isaiah 42 cannot be applied to an Israelite prophet because Kedar is a son of Ishmael (p. 63). His argument is flawed in the following ways:

- Using this logic, Isaiah 42 cannot refer to Muhammad because "Sela" is the naturally fortified capital of the Edomites south of the Dead Sea. The Edomites are the sons of Jacob's brother Esau, who was in turn a son of Isaac, not Ishmael.
- What Isaiah 42:11 is saying is not that God's promised Servant would come from the villages of Kedar or from Sela, but rather, that all peoples, including the Ishmaelites and Edomites, would be able to rejoice at His coming, for He would bring salvation and redemption to all, through grace by faith.

i. *"Declaring God's Praise" in the Islands Refers to Small Islands that Converted to Islam*

Dr. Baagil argues that Isaiah 42:12 ("Let them give glory to the Lord, and declare His praise in the coastlands"), which is sometimes translated as "praise in the islands," is a reference to Islam, which "spread to the small islands as far as Indonesia and the Caribbean Sea" (p. 63).

While it is true that some islands, such as Indonesia, are Muslim-majority, the Islands of the Caribbean are Christian-majority. And if the religion of islands is the criterion to which Isaiah 42:12 is deemed applicable, then Christianity qualifies, as it has reached not only small islands (*e.g.*, St. Thomas, St. Martin, Bermuda and other islands of the Caribbean), but large islands as well (*e.g.*, Australia).

j. *Muhammad "Prevailed against His Enemies"*

Finally, Dr. Baagil argues that Isaiah 42:13 ("He shall prevail against His enemies") is an indication that the prophecy refers to Muhammad, because "In a short period the Kingdom of God on earth was established with the advent of Muhammad" (p 64). However, the same can be said of Jesus, who not only prevailed against His enemies and conquered sin and death, but also gives victory to His followers (1Co 15:55-58).

8. Muhammad as David's "Lord"

a. *Dr. Baagil's Argument*

Dr. Baagil quotes Psalm 110:1: "The Lord said to my Lord, 'Sit at My right hand, Till I make Your enemies Your footstool'" and argues that the second "Lord" is Muhammad. He argues that if the first "Lord" is God, then the second "Lord" cannot be God, because David knew only one God. The Church believes the second "Lord" to be Jesus, but this is not possible because of Jesus' words in Luke 20:42-44, "David himself said in the Book of Psalms: 'The Lord said to my Lord,' sit at my right hand ... Therefore David calls Him 'Lord'; how is He then his Son?" Dr. Baagil concludes that the second "Lord" cannot be Jesus because Jesus was David's son, and a father cannot call a son "Lord."

So who was the second "Lord"? Dr. Baagil points to the Gospel of Barnabas for the answer. He writes that the Gospel of Barnabas mentioned explicitly "that the promise was made in Ishmael, not in Isaac. David's Lord was thus Muhammad [PBUH] whom he [David] saw in spirit. No Prophet ever accomplished more than Muhammad [PBUH]. Even the work of all other Prophets together is still small compared with what Muhammad [PBUH] did within a short period of 23 years, and which remains unchanged until now" (p. 64).

b. Flaws in Dr. Baagil's Argument

Dr. Baagil's Argument is flawed for the following reasons:

i. David's "Lord" Is the "Messiah"

Jesus asked the Sadducees, "How can they say that the Christ is the Son of David?" (Luke 20:41). He was referring to a Jewish tradition that recognized that the promised Messiah (the Christ), would come from David's line. Jesus asks how the Messiah could be David's son if David himself calls the Messiah "Lord"; in Jewish culture, it is the father, not the son, who receives such honor.

However, all of this changes in the case of Jesus, who is who was more than just a an earthly savior; He was also the divine Son of God. In asking the Sadducees how David could call His son "Lord," Jesus was challenging the Sadducees to grapple with His divinity, which Jesus repeatedly affirmed (e.g., when the high priest asked Jesus, "Tell us if You are the Christ, the Son of God!" (Mat 26:63), Jesus answered, "It is as you said" (Mat 26:64); similarly, when Jesus asked His disciples, "Who do men say that I, the Son of Man, am," Simon Peter answered and said, "You are the Christ, the Son of the living God," Jesus replied and said to him, "Blessed are you, Simon Bar-Jonah, for flesh and blood has not revealed this to you, but My Father who is in heaven" (Mat 16:13-17)). In other words, David was able to call his son Jesus "Lord" because Jesus was the son of God.

ii. Muhammad was Not the Christ

In the passage that Dr. Baagil quotes, Jesus was specifically asking about the "Christ." Jesus wrote, "How can they say that the *Christ* is the Son of David?" (Luke 20:41). Jesus was exploring how the promised Messiah could be David's son, if David called him Lord. Dr. Baagil finds the answer in Muhammad: David is able to call Muhammad "Lord" because Muhammad was not a son of David; rather, he was a son of Ishmael. The logical implication to this, then, is that Muhammad is the promised savior (the Christ) that the Jews had been waiting for.

This is truly ironic, because even Muslims do not consider Muhammad to be the Messiah of the Jews. Muhammad brought neither spiritual nor physical salvation to the Jews. The true irony of this is the fact that in the modern geo-politic, Muslims are the greatest enemies of the Jews, having vehemently opposed the creation of Israel and having launched countless wars against Israel since its foundation. The cooperation between Nazi Germany and Arab world was in part founded on a common enemy, Jews, Zionism and Judaism, though it was also partly founded in Arabs' hope that Nazi Germany would free them from the rule of colonial France and Great Britain. Nonetheless, Hitler won support in the Arab world, as evidenced most notably by the cooperation between the Grand Mufti of Jerusalem Hajj Amin al-Husseini, who collaborated with the Nazis.

Dr. Baagil's suggestion that Muhammad was the Messiah that David prophesied about is most ironic in light of the witness of the *Qur'an* itself, which repeatedly calls Jesus, *not* Muhammad, the Messiah:

-   *Surah* 3:44: "O Mary, surely *Allah* gives thee good news with a word from Him (of one) whose name is the Messiah, Jesus, son of Mary" (اسْمُهُ الْمَسِيحُ عِيسَى ابْنُ مَرْيَمَ)؛
-   *Surah* 4:157: "We have killed the Messiah, Jesus, son of Mary" (الْمَسِيحَ عِيسَى ابْنَ مَرْيَمَ)؛
-   *Surah* 4:171: "The Messiah, Jesus, son of Mary, is only a messenger of *Allah* and His word" (إِنَّمَا الْمَسِيحُ عِيسَى ابْنُ مَرْيَمَ).
-   *Surah* 5:75: "The Messiah, son of Mary, was only a messenger" (الْمَسِيحُ ابْنُ مَرْيَمَ)؛ etc.

c. *Problems with the Gospel of Barnabas*

Dr. Baagil argues that Muhammad is David's "Lord" because according to the Gospel of Barnabas, "the promise was made in Ishmael, not in Isaac. David's Lord was thus Muhammad ... No Prophet ever accomplished more than Muhammad [PBUH]" (p. 64).

There are several flaws in this argument:

i. The Gospel of Barnabas Is of Questionable Authenticity

According to Answering-Islam.org,[6] reputable scholars have carefully examined the Gospel of Barnabas and find no basis for its authenticity. After reviewing the evidence in an article in Islamochristiana, the annual scientific periodical dedicated to Christian-Muslim dialogue, J. Slomp concluded that "in my opinion scholarly research has proved absolutely that this 'gospel' is a fake. This opinion is also held by a number of Muslim scholars" ("The Gospel in Dispute," in *Islamochristiana* (Rome: Pontificio Instituto di Studi Arabi, 1978), vol. 4, 68).

In their introduction to the Oxford edition of *The Gospel of Barnabas*, Longsdale and Ragg write that "the true date lies ... nearer to the sixteenth century than to the first [century]" (*The Gospel of Barnabas* (Oxford: Clarendon Press, 1907), xxxvii). Moreover, in his classic work "Jomier proved his point by showing beyond any doubt that the G. B. V. contains an islamicised late medieval gospel forgery" (J. Jomier, *Egypte: Reflexions sur la Recontre al-Azhar* (Vatican au Caire, 1978), cited by Slomp, 104) (see <www.answering-islam.org/Barnabas/saleeb.html> for further treatment of the Gospel of Barnabas).

ii. Even if God Made His Covenant with Ishmael, Muhammad is not David's "Lord"

Yet even if the Gospel of Barnabas is true, Muhammad would not become David's "Lord." All it means is that God made a covenant with Ishmael whereby if he kept God's laws and performed ritual sacrifices, God would give to Ishmael a promised land. In other words, all of the promises that God made to Israel (Jacob) should instead be interpreted as promises made to Ishmael. This is quite ironic because the land allegedly promised to Ishmael is today occupied by the descendants of Israel (Jacob), not Ishmael. Moreover, it is indeed very

---

[6] Available at <www.answering-islam.org/Barnabas/saleeb.html>.

strange that God would promise to Ishmael a spiritual savior who came from the line of Isaac through David, one who brought salvation "for the Jew first and also for the Gentile" (Rom 1:16), rather than to the Arab first. Yet even if we accepted all of these illogical arguments and accepted the Gospel of Barnabas as authentic, Muhammad still would not be deemed David's divine "Lord."

d. Jesus' Miracles Eclipse Muhammad's Military Victories

Dr. Baagil writes that "Even the work of all other Prophets together is still small compared with what Muhammad [PBUH] did within a short period of 23 years" (p. 64). This statement is flawed in the following respects:

- A prophet's greatness is relative to the criteria applied by the measurer. If military might and conquest is the criterion to be applied, then Muhammad was arguably great: With the sword, he conquered the Arabian Gulf and Levant and later, through his followers, Anatolia, Central Asia, North Africa and the Iberian Peninsula.

- Yet even if military might is the standard to be applied, Moses is arguably greater because though his wonders and miracles, he took an unarmed slave nation from the great Egyptian Pharaoh Thutmoses III and with only a staff, divided the Red Sea for the Israelites to cross (Exo 14:21) and then closed the sea over Pharaoh's chariots and horsemen (Exo 14:26). This is, at least from the supernatural perspective, far more impressive than Muhammad's conquest of Christian and Jewish civilians living in the Levant and the Jewish holy lands.

- By other standards, such as wonders and miracles, other prophets far eclipse Muhammad. For example, the prophet Elisha had such a great portion of the Holy Spirit that when a dead man was let down into Elisah's tomb, he suddenly revived and stood on his feet upon touching the bones of Elisha (2Ki 13:21).

- Another criterion could be salvation. Only Jesus has brought salvation through the forgiveness of sins by his own sacrifice. He has opened up the doors of salvation and conquered sin and death (1Co 15:55-58) as no other man has done.

e. Muhammad's Work Remains Unchanged Until Now

Finally, Dr. Baagil argues that Muhammad's work "remains unchanged until now" (p. 64). While it is true that most of the territories that Muhammad conquered remain Muslim through the imposition of laws that punish converts and prohibit non-Muslim places of worship (*e.g.*, in Saudi Arabia), Muhammad's work has not remained "unchanged" in other territories that he conquered. The most obvious example is modern Palestine, which was once conquered by Islam but is now the site of modern-day Israel.

9. Muhammad as the Prophet that the Jews Asked John the Baptist About

a. Dr. Baagil's Argument

Dr. Baagil quotes John's reply to the priests and Levites who were sent from Jerusalem to ask him who he was. "He confessed, and did not deny, but confessed, 'I am not the Christ.' And they asked him, 'What then? Are you Elijah?' He said, 'I am not.' 'Are you the Prophet?' And he answered, 'No' (John 1:20-21).

Dr. Baagil interprets the distinction that the Jews made between the "Prophet" and the "Christ" as an indication that there was a "Prophet" that the Jews expected who was distinct from the Messiah. Dr. Baagil asks, "Was he not the one like unto Moses (Deuteronomy 18:18) who is Muhammad [PBUH]?" (p. 65).

b. Flaw in Argument

i. Muhammad Cannot Be the Promised Prophet

Dr. Baagil is correct in one respect: The "Prophet" that the priests and Levites asked John the Baptist about was the Prophet of Deuteronomy 18:18 ("I will raise up for them a Prophet like you from among their brethren, and will put My words in His mouth, and He shall speak to them all that I command Him"). However, as already discussed under "Muhammad is the Prophet Like unto Moses," above, Muhammad cannot be this prophet:

- The Prophet like Moses was to come from among the Israelites, not the Ishmaelites;
- The Prophet like Moses is a reference to a line of prophets;
- The Prophet must be "like unto Moses," but the similarities between Moses and Muhammad are limited.

ii.   Confusion as to Who John the Baptist and Jesus Were

Before jumping to any conclusion as to who the prophet referred to by the Jews in John 1:20-21, it is first necessary to understand the times and context of the inquiry. The Jews always expected prophets to appear from God throughout their history, in keeping with God's promise in Deuteronomy 18:18. Throughout their history, the Jews had prophets to guide them and keep them accountable—from Moses to Elijah to Elisha to Isaiah to Jeremiah to Daniel to Jonah to Malachi and many others. When Malachi had promised the sending of Elijah the prophet "before the coming of the great and dreadful day of the Lord" (Mal 4:5-6), the Jews waited in anxious anticipation for the return of Elijah. Yet a long 400 years passed before the coming of the next prophet, John the Baptist. At the time of John the Baptist, the Jews went through a progressive spiritual decline, having gone centuries without hearing a word from the Lord. Many waited in anxious expectation for another prophet in the line of Deuteronomy 18:18; for the return of Elijah in keeping with Malachi 4:5-6; and for the coming of the Messiah.

When both Jesus and John the Baptist came, there was confusion as to who they both were. John 1:20-21 clearly expresses this confusion: The Jews did not know whether John was the Deuteronomy 18:18 prophet; Elijah; or the Messiah. There is similar confusion as to who Jesus was. Herod believed Jesus was John the Baptist, resurrected from the dead (Mark 6:14). Others believed that John the Baptist was Elijah or one of the Deuteronomy 18:18 prophets (Mark 6:15). When Jesus asked His disciples, "Who do men say that I am?" (Mark 8:27), they answered, "John the Baptist; but some say, Elijah; and others, one of the prophets" (Mark 8:28).

It is within this context, with Jews in a state of spiritual decline, unable to recognize John the Baptist, who Jesus repeatedly said fulfilled the return of Elijah (Mat 11:14 ("he is Elijah who is to come"); Mat 17:12-13 (Jesus said, "'I say to you that Elijah has come already' ... the disciples understood that He spoke to them of John the Baptist"), or Jesus, the promised Christ (Messiah) (Mark 8:29-30).

John the Baptist denied that he was the Deuteronomy 18:18 prophet, Elijah and the Christ. Yet this does not mean that Muhammad was any of these things. Muhammad could not be the Deuteronomy 18:18 for the reasons enumerated above (see "Muhammad is the Prophet Like unto Moses"). Muhammad was not Elijah, who was to come, because John fulfilled the Malachi 4:5 prophecy about Elijah's return, as spoken by Jesus in Matthew 11:14 and Matthew 17:12-13 (whether Elijah will physically return before "the coming of the great and dreadful day of the Lord" of Malachi 4:5 is another question. Finally, he was not the Christ (Messiah) because Jesus fulfilled this role, as attested by the *Qur'an* itself (*Surah* 3:44; *Surah* 4:157; *Surah* 4:171; *Surah* 5:75).

10. Muhammad as the Baptizer with Holy Ghost and with Fire

a. Dr. Baagil's Argument

Next, Dr. Baagil argues that Muhammad is the one referenced by John the Baptist when he said "I indeed baptize you with water unto repentance, but He who is coming after me is mightier than I, whose sandals I am not worthy to carry. He will baptize you with the Holy Spirit and fire" (Mat 3:11). Dr. Baagil writes (p. 65):

> If Jesus was alluded to here, John the Baptist would not go back to live in the jungle again, but to cling to him and be one of his disciples, which he did not do. So another powerful Prophet was here alluded to, and not Jesus. The one coming after John the Baptist could not be Jesus as both were contemporaries. Here again, was is not Prophet Muhammad [PBUH] alluded to by John the Baptist?

b. Flaws in Argument

There are several flaws in Dr. Baagil's argument:

i.   John the Baptist Neither Lived in Nor Returned to the Jungle

Dr. Baagil first argues that if "Jesus was alluded to here, John the Baptist would not go back to live in the jungle again" (p. 65). Dr. Baagil is perhaps confused here. He states that John the Baptist would not have gone back to the "jungle," yet John the Baptist neither lived in nor returned to the jungle. Rather, John the Baptist preached in the wilderness of Judea (Mat 3:1) and baptized in the Jordan River (Mat 3:6; Mark 1:5; etc.).

ii. John the Baptist Was Called to be the Forerunner of Christ, not a Disciple

Dr. Baagil states that if John the Baptist preached the coming of Jesus, then John would "cling to him and be one of his disciples" (p.

65). Yet John the Baptist was not called to be a disciple. Rather, he was called to be the forerunner of Christ, fulfilling the words of Isaiah: "the voice of one crying in the wilderness: 'prepare the way of the Lord; make his paths straight'" (Mat 3:3). Jesus called each disciple for a specific reason, some were even uneducated and untrained (Acts 4:13), to manifest the glory of God. Jesus did not call John the Baptist to be a disciple because John the Baptist was called to fulfill a different role, that of the forerunner of Christ, who would prepare the way for salvation by preaching a baptism of repentance for the remission of sins (Mark 1:4).

After Jesus was baptized (Mark 1:11), the Holy Spirit immediately drove Him into the wilderness (Mark 1:12), where He was tempted by Satan for forty days (Mark 1:13). It is relatively clear that John the Baptist did not follow Jesus, because the Scriptures say only that Jesus was with the wild beasts, and the angels ministered to Him (Mark 1:13). Yet if John the Baptist stayed behind, this cannot be read as an indication that Jesus was not the one that John preached about. John most likely remained behind to continue his work in preaching the road to salvation, until he was put in prison, at which point Jesus came to Galilee to preach the gospel of the kingdom of God (Mark 1:14). If they were separated, it was likely because God wished for John to be present preaching the kingdom of God, while Jesus was tested and strengthened in the wilderness, with Jesus taking John's place after John was imprisoned, *not* because John rejected or otherwise did not consider Jesus to be the one whose path he was preparing.

iii. Because John the Baptist was the Forerunner of the Lord, the One He Spoke About was Jesus Christ, Not Muhammad

Dr. Baagil casually concludes that John the Baptist prophesied the coming of Muhammad, but such a conclusion is illogical in light of both John the Baptist's words and the prophecies about him:

- Malachi prophesied of John the Baptist: The Lord spoke, "Behold, I send My messenger, and he will prepare the way before Me. And the Lord, whom you seek, will suddenly come to His temple, Even the Messenger of the covenant, In whom you delight" (Mal 3:1);
- Isaiah prophesies of John the Baptist as "the *voice of one crying in the wilderness*: 'Prepare the way of the LORD; *Make straight in the desert a highway for our God*'" (Isa 40:3);

- Mark attributes both of these prophesies to John (Mark 1:2-3);
- John the Baptist attributes Isaiah's words to himself: "I am '*the voice of one crying in the wilderness*: "*make straight the way of the Lord*"'" (John 1:23)

These Scriptures make clear that the one that John the Baptist prophesied of was more than just a man or a prophet; He was the "Lord." Muslims never claim that Muhammad is Lord, but Christians do, on the basis of:

- Multiple New Testament declarations that He is God (*e.g.*, John 1:1; Tit 2:13; etc.);
- Jesus' various affirmations of His divinity (Mat 26:63-64; Mat 16:13-17);
- Jesus' claiming of the Divine Name for Himself (John 8:58);
- Old Testament prophecy that the Messiah will be God (Isa 9:6);
- Jesus' titles belonging only to God (*e.g.*, Isa 44:6; Rev 1:17; Rev 17:14; etc.); and
- The Jews' understanding that Jesus claimed to be the Son of God (John 10:33; John 8:58-59).

Because John the Baptist preached the coming of the "Lord," he could only be speaking of Jesus, the Son of God, not Muhammad, a mere mortal man.

iv. The One John the Baptist Alluded to Baptizes in the Holy Spirit and Fire, But Muhammad Never Baptized Anyone

(1) Overview

The One John the Baptist alluded to baptizes in the Holy Spirit and fire, but Muhammad baptized in neither the Holy Spirit nor in fire. Jesus, in contrast, baptized in the Holy Spirit and in fire. Jesus is therefore the one to whom John the Baptist alluded.

(2) Jesus Baptized in the Holy Spirit

The Scripture makes clear that it is Jesus who baptizes in the Holy Spirit. John the Baptist declared that "He who sent me to baptize in water said to me, 'He upon whom you see the Spirit descending and remaining upon Him, this is the one who baptizes in the Holy Spirit'"

(John 1:33). John the Baptist saw the Spirit descend and remain on Jesus (John 1:32; Mat 3:16; Luke 3:22), not on Muhammad.

Jesus promised His disciples that He would send the Holy Spirit:

- Jesus will "pray the Father, and He will give you another Helper, that He may abide with you forever—the Spirit of truth" (John 14:16-17);
- "The Helper, the Holy Spirit, whom the Father will send in My name, He will teach you all things" (John 14:26);
- "But when the Helper comes, whom I shall send to you from the Father, the Spirit of truth who proceeds from the Father, He will testify of Me" (John 15:26).
- "Being assembled together with them, He commanded them not to depart from Jerusalem, but to wait for the Promise of the Father, which, He said, you have heard from Me; for John truly baptized with water, but you shall be baptized with the Holy Spirit not many days from now" (Acts 1:4).

The fulfillment of the promise of the Holy Spirit came on Pentecost:

"Suddenly there came a sound from heaven, as of a rushing mighty wind, and it filled the whole house where they were sitting. Then there appeared to them divided tongues, as of fire, and one sat upon each of them. And they were all filled with the Holy Spirit and began to speak with other tongues, as the Spirit gave them utterance" (Acts 2:2-4), in fulfillment of the prophecy of Joel: "And it shall come to pass afterward That I will pour out My Spirit on all flesh; Your sons and your daughters shall prophesy, Your old men shall dream dreams, Your young men shall see visions" (Joe 2:28; Acts 2:17).

Jesus both promised and gave the Holy Spirit; Muhammad neither promised nor gave the Holy Spirit. Therefore, John the Baptist's allusion to one who would "baptize in the Holy Spirit" must be interpreted as a reference to Jesus, not to Muhammad.

(3) Jesus Baptizes with Fire

John the Baptist declared that the one coming after him will baptize with "fire" (Mat 3:11). Baptism of fire is an allusion not to the receipt of the Holy Spirit, but of judgment. John the Baptist makes this clear in both the verses preceding and succeeding his reference to baptism. He proclaims that "every tree which does not bear good fruit is cut down and thrown into the fire" (Mat 3:10) and that the one to come after him "will thoroughly clean out His threshing floor, and gather His wheat into the barn; but He will burn up the chaff with unquenchable fire" (Mat 3:12). One sees here the dichotomy between the "wheat," which will be gathered into the barn, and the chaff, to be thrown into unquenchable fire, which parallels the baptism of the Holy Spirit, reserved for believers bearing good fruit, and the baptism of fire, reserved for sinners who reject God's grace and salvation.

The association of fire with judgment appears throughout the Scriptures. For example, the "beast" and "false prophet" were "cast alive into the lake of fire" (Rev 19:20). Therefore, the one who baptizes in fire must have the authority to judge good and evil. Muhammad was a mere man with no authority to judge sinners and the righteous. Jesus, in contrast, was the Son of God who sits at the judgment seat which we all will stand before (Rom 14:10; 2Co 5:10).

11. Muhammad as the Promised "Comforter"

a. Introduction

Dr. Baagil quotes Jesus' promise at John 14:16: "I will pray the Father, and he shall give you another Comforter, that he may abide with you forever." Dr. Baagil claims that we "do not know exactly the original Aramaic word used by Jesus for Comforter. Other Bibles use Consoler, Advocate, Helper, and in Greek Bibles the word *Paraclete*. There are different explanations for it: Holy Spirit, the Word, a person, etc." (p. 66). In the pages following, Dr. Baagil argues that the original Greek should be understood to refer to Muhammad.

In the following sections, we will first explore the original Greek of "Comforter" as well as the context of John 14:16 to fully understand its meaning. We will then explore the eight arguments that Dr. Baagil offers to try to prove that the "Comforter" is Muhammad, and will refute each argument in turn.

b. The Meaning of "Comforter" (παράκλητος / paraklētos)

i. The Five Instances of the Greek Work παράκλητος (*paraklētos*) in the Bible

Jesus begins his discussion of the "Comforter" by saying (John 14:15-16, NKJV):

If you love Me, keep My commandments. And I will pray the Father, and He will give you another Helper, that He may abide with you forever.

The word that Jesus used here for "Comforter" or "Helper" is the Greek παράκλητος (*paraklētos*, G3875), which is variously translated into English as "Comforter" (ASV, Darby, KJV, MKJV), "Helper" (BBE, ESV, ISV, NKJV) and "Counselor" (NIV, RSV).

The Greek παράκλητος appears five times in the Bible. In all five cases, it appears in writings (the Gospel of John and 1 John) authored by John. In the following verses, taken from the NKJV, it is translated as "Helper" or "Advocate":

- John 14:16: "And I will pray the Father, and He will give you another **Helper**, that He may abide with you forever";
- John 14:26: "John 14:26 But the **Helper**, the Holy Spirit, whom the Father will send in My name, He will teach you all things, and bring to your remembrance all things that I said to you";
- John 15:26: "But when the **Helper** comes, whom I shall send to you from the Father, the Spirit of truth who proceeds from the Father, He will testify of Me";
- John 16:7: "Nevertheless I tell you the truth. It is to your advantage that I go away; for if I do not go away, the **Helper** will not come to you; but if I depart, I will send Him to you";
- 1Jn 2:1: "My little children, these things I write to you, so that you may not sin. And if anyone sins, we have an **Advocate** with the Father, Jesus Christ the righteous."

These five instances of the word *paraklētos* can be summarized as follows:

- In four instances in John in which Jesus uses the term *paraklētos*. Based on the context, as discussed below, we can conclude that Jesus was referring to the Holy Spirit when he stated *paraklētos*.
- In one instance in 1 John in which John used the term *paraklētos* to unequivocally refer to Jesus.

In total, the Greek παράκλητος is applied to the Holy Spirit four times as one who helps and teaches and once to Jesus as an advocate who intercedes for sinners before the Father. We can thus conclude that the original Greek refers to any person who helps someone in trouble. We find this meaning in *Thayer's Lexicon*, which defines παράκλητος as one who is "summoned, called to one's side, esp. called to one's aid" and "in the widest sense, a helper, succourer, aider, assistant." The word also has a legal side, as "one who pleads another's cause before a judge, a pleader, counsel for defense."

ii. The Meaning of παράκλητος (*Paraklētos*) in John 14:16 Is Made Evident by the Verses that Follow

We can determine whether the *paraklētos* as used in John 14:16 is applicable to the Holy Spirit or to Muhammad by examining the verses following John 14:16 in the Gospel of John. These verses make clear that the *paraklētos* is a spirit rather than a physical person.

(1) John 14:17 and John 15:26 Attest that the "Comforter" is a "Spirit"

John 14:17 and John 15:26 make clear that the "comforter" is a "spirit," not a person:

- John 14:17 ("the *Spirit of truth*, whom the world cannot receive, because it neither sees Him nor knows Him; but you know Him, for He dwells with you and will be in you") states that the Comforter is "the Spirit of truth" that the world does not "see," but rather, that "dwells" in Jesus' followers.
- John 15:26 states that the Comforter (here translated as "Helper") is "*the Spirit of truth* who proceeds from the Father."

John 14:17 and 15:26 thus make it clear that the Comforter (Helper, Counselor, etc.) is an unseen spirit. The Comforter therefore cannot be Muhammad, who was a mere man who was seen and composed of flesh and bone.

(2) John 14:17 Makes Clear that the *Paraklētos* "Dwells in You"

John 14:17 further makes clear that the *paraklētos* "dwells with you and will be in you" (John 14:17). This parallels the coming of the Holy Spirit on Pentecost, when the disciples were "all filled with the Holy Spirit" (Acts 2:4). That the Holy Spirit is the John 14:17 *paraklētos* that dwells in us is made clear by Romans 8:9: "you are not in the flesh but in the Spirit, if indeed the Spirit of God dwells in you." Through the Holy Spirit, we are in Jesus, just as Jesus is "in My

Father" (John 14:20). None of these words can be said about Muhammad, who does not "dwell" in the people of God as the *parakletos* (Holy Spirit) does.

iii. John 14:26 Equates the Comforter with the "Holy Spirit"

John 14:26 makes it explicitly clear that the *parakletos* (translated "Helper" in the NKJV) is the Holy Spirit because it equates the two: "But the Helper [*parakletos*], the Holy Spirit, whom the Father will send in My name, He will teach you all things." Here, the clause "Holy Spirit" refers back to "Helper," which is the NKJV translation of the Greek παράκλητος (*parakletos*).

c. *Dr. Baagil's Arguments that Muhammad is the* Parakletos *and Responses*

i. Muhammad was "Another Comforter"

Jesus says that the Father "will give you *another* Comforter" (John 14:16). Dr. Baagil writes that "So many Comforters had come and another one was to come" (p. 67). This does not, of course, establish any more that the Comforter was Muhammad than that it was the Holy Spirit or some other later figure to later claim prophethood (*e.g.*, Guru Nanak, Joseph Smith, Bahá'u'lláh, etc.).

What Jesus meant is made evident later in the Gospel of John, specifically, in John 14:26, which equates the *parakletos* with the Holy Spirit:

> But the Helper [*parakletos*], the Holy Spirit, whom the Father will send in My name, He will teach you all things, and bring to your remembrance all things that I said to you.

With these words, Jesus is conveying that he would send to the disciples the Holy Spirit, who would take Jesus' place in teaching the disciples all things and leading them to all truth (John 14:26).

ii. Muhammad, the "Seal of all Prophets," Abides with Us Forever

Jesus states that the Comforter will "abide with you forever" (John 14:16). According to Dr. Baagil, this is a reference to Muhammad because (p. 67):

there was no need for another one to come after him, and he was the Seal of all Prophets. The teaching will abide forever, will remain intact.

There are several problems with Dr. Baagil's argument:

- Dr. Baagil believes that in writing of a Comforter who would "abide with you forever" (John 14:16), the Apostle John, who wrote the Gospel of John, meant that another prophet, Muhammad, would come along and add to Jesus' prophecy, "sealing" it forever. This is ironic in light of the words of the Book of Revelation, also written by the Apostle John, which warn (Rev 22:18):
  I testify to everyone who hears *the words of the prophecy of this book*: If anyone adds to these things, God will add to him the plagues that are written in this book; and if anyone takes away from the words of the book of this prophecy, God shall take away his part from the Book of Life, from the holy city, and from the things which are written in this book.

  How then we can we explain that on the one hand, John warns those who add to the words of the Bible with new prophecies, but on the other hand, he writes of the coming of one who would later come and change the words spoken in the Bible?
- John writes of one who will "abide with you forever." Muhammad died at the age of 62 or 63. The Holy Spirit, in contrast, is one with the immortal God ("Now the Lord is the Spirit" (2Co 3:17); see also Acts 5:3-4, equating the Holy Spirit with God), and thus abides forever.
- The fact that Muhammad's teaching (as recorded in the *Qur'an*) "remain intact" and unchanged does not mean that John the Apostle was referring to Muhammad. The teachings of the Holy Spirit, as revealed in the Bible by inspired writers, also remains intact, as do the teachings of others who have claimed to be prophets. For example, the writings of Bahá'u'lláh remain intact and unchanged to this day, yet followers of the Baha'i faith do not claim that Bahá'u'lláh is the *paraklētos* in John 14:16.

iii. Only Muhammad Reproved the "World" of Sin

Dr. Baagil states that Muhammad is the *paraklētos* because Jesus says that the *paraklētos* will "convict [reprove] the world of sin" (John 16:8). Dr. Baagil argues that (p. 67):

> all other Prophets, even Abraham, Moses, David and Solomon chastised their neighbors and their people for sin, but not the world as Muhammad [PBUH] did.

The discussion of other prophets is irrelevant here because Christians do not claim that the *paraklētos* is a prophet; they claim, in accordance with the clear meaning of John 14:16, 26, 15:26, 16:7 and 1Jn 2:1, that the *paraklētos* is the Holy Spirit. It is indeed the Holy Spirit that convicts the world of sin. When one receives the Holy Spirit, he becomes aware of his sinful nature and the need of God's grace unto salvation. The Holy Spirit does not convict only His "neighbors" of sin, but the world, for He was given not only to the Jews, but also to the Gentiles and to all nations where believers profess Christ is Lord.

iv. Muhammad Judged the "Prince of the World"

Jesus states that "the ruler of this world is judged" (John 16:11). This, of course, means that Satan is judged (see John 14:30, which equates the "ruler of this world" with one who has nothing in Jesus), but it does not state that it is the *paraklētos* who judges Satan. Rather, it is Jesus who sits at the judgment seat (Rom 14:10; 2Co 5:10).

Yet even if John 16:11 were stating that the *paraklētos* judges Satan, Muhammad cannot then be the *paraklētos* because he has no authority to judge good and evil, for this authority is reserved for God alone.

v. Muhammad was the "Spirit of Truth"

Dr. Baagil argues that Muhammad is the John 16:13 "Spirit of truth" because "[s]ince childhood Prophet Muhammad [PBUH] was called Al-Ameen, i.e. the Honest or Truthful One" (p. 67-68). There are several problems with this argument:

-   First, John 16:13 states that the Comforter is the "Spirit of truth." The Holy Spirit is a spirit, but Muhammad a physical person.

- Second, there are historical accounts that suggest that Muhammad permitted deceit in certain circumstances, such as in the case of war. He said, for example, "War is deceit" (narrated Jabir bin 'Abdullah, Vol. 4, Book 52, No. 269). When Muhammad requested a volunteer to assassinate Ka'b bin al-Ashraf, one of his followers volunteered and asked Muhammad to "allow me to say a (false) thing (i.e. to deceive Ka'b)." Muhammad answered "You may say it" (*Bukhari*, Vol. 5, No. 369, Narrated by Jabir Abdullah). While it is debatable whether the assassination of Ka'b bin al-Ashraf was justified, the condoning of deceit casts into question whether Muhammad can be the "Spirit of truth" that the Apostle John wrote about.

vi. Muhammad Spoke Not of His Own Authority, but of God's

John writes that the Comforter "will not speak on His own authority, but whatever He hears He will speak; and He will tell you things to come" (John 16:13). Dr. Baagil interprets this to point to Muhammad because "[t]he Holy *Qur'an* is God's Word. Not a single word from Prophet Muhammad [PBUH] or his companions was included" (p. 68).

The follower of any religion could state the same about his own holy book and derive the same conclusion. In fact, most religious people believe their religious books contain the unadulterated Word of God. The obstacle that Dr. Baagil must overcome is proving that the *Qur'an*, which repeatedly contradicts God's Word in the Bible, indeed records God's Word.

vii. All of Muhammad's Prophecies Came to Pass

The Comforter "will tell you things to come" (John 16:13). Dr. Baagil concludes that the Comforter is Muhammad, since "[a]ll prophecies of Prophet Muhammad [PBUH] came to pass" (p. 68). However, Dr. Baagil gives no evidence of prophecies that Prophet Muhammad spoke that later came to pass. The Holy Spirit, in contrast, continues to "tell you things to come" through the gift of prophecy, which is one of the gifts of the Holy Spirit (1Co 12:1-11).

viii.   Muhammad Glorified God More than the Bible and Christians Do

Jesus declares that the Comforter "will glorify Me" (John 16:14). Muhammad argues that the Comforter must then be Muhammad, who has "more reverence for Jesus (PBUH) than the Bible and Christians themselves" (p. 68). This is truly ironic, because Christians and the Bible profess that Jesus was the Son of God (John 1:1; Mat 26:73-64), who is worthy of praise and receiving of the honors that the Father receives (John 5:23), who had the power to forgive sin (Mat 9:2), who sits at the right hand of the Father (Heb 1:3), is superior to the angels (Heb 1:4) and sits at the judgment seat (Rom 14:10; 2Co 5:10). Muhammad, in contrast, demotes Jesus to a mere man, a mortal who is less in honor than even Muhammad and strips Him of the New Testament titles "Son of God" (*e.g.*, Mat 26:63-64), "God" and "Savior" (*e.g.*, Tit 2:13).

To this, Dr. Baagil would offer the following arguments, each of which is summarized and refuted below:

(1) To Believe in his Death on the Cross Discredits His Prophethood

Deuteronomy 13:5 declares that "that prophet or that dreamer of dreams shall be put to death." Dr. Baagil concludes then that believing that Jesus died on the cross "discredits his prophethood" (p. 68). Yet Dr. Baagil's conclusion is based on a complete misunderstanding of Deuteronomy 13:5. The verse does not mean that every prophet who is put to death is a false prophet. If so, then we must conclude that every prophet that the Jews killed, including Zechariah (2Ch 24:20-22) and Uriah (Jer 26:20-23), was a false prophet. Of course, they were not false prophets, and even the *Qur'an* recognizes that Jews put their own prophets to death: "they disbelieved in the messages of God and would kill the prophets unjustly" (*Surah* 2:61).

Rather, what Deuteronomy 13:5 is stating is that the Jews were to put to death false prophets. Yet the fact that the Jews, in their sin, put to death true prophets, does not mean that the person put to death is a false prophet; it simply means that the Jews, like all of mankind, are sinful.

As for Dr. Baagil's suggestion that Jesus could not have been crucified because "he that is hanged is accursed of God" according to Deuteronomy 21:22 (p. 68), we have already shown how Jesus "redeemed us from the curse of the law, having become a curse for us" (Gal 3:13), discussed above (see "He Who Hangs on a Tree is Accursed of God").

(2) Jesus Could Not Have Cried Out "My God, my God, Why hast Thou Forsaken Me"

As He hung on the cross, Jesus cried out, "My God, My God, why have You forsaken Me?" (Mat 27:46). Dr. Baagil concludes that this could not have been Jesus on the cross because "[e]ven a non-Prophet would smile at agony as he knew that his death would win him the title of martyr. Was this not an insult to Jesus in not having faith in *Allah*?" (p. 68).

Here, Dr. Baagil misses several important points and misreads the Scripture:

-   Jesus' death symbolized not only the sacrifice of a martyr, but the crucifixion of the Son of God to bear all of the sins of the world. His cry indicates to us the weight of the burden he bore, one not comparable to an ordinary earthly death.
-   Jesus cried out to God in fulfillment of Psalm 22:1, which captures David's cry to God as he was persecuted by long and vicious attacks that he had not provoked. Jesus' call to God and his circumstances parallel those of David, just as the division of Jesus' garments (John 19:23-24) parallel and fulfill the prophecy of Psalm 22:18.
-   Jesus was both God and man. As such, he experienced suffering as a man. His cries out to God thus reflected the pain and suffering of a man who had experienced unspeakable torture, lashings and crucifixion.

(3) Jesus Could Not Label the Gentiles as Dogs and Swine and Address his Mother as Woman

Finally, Dr. Baagil argues that "[w]e Muslims cannot believe that Jesus could label the Gentiles as dogs and swine and address his mother with Woman, as the Holy Qur'an states in Surah 19:32: 'And dutiful to my Mother [i.e. Mary], and [*Allah*] made me not an unblessed and arrogant'" (p. 68-69). We will take each argument in turn.

(a) "Do not give what is holy to the dogs; nor cast your pearls before swine"

It is ironic that, according to Dr. Baagil, "Muslims cannot believe that Jesus could label the Gentiles as dogs and swine" when Muslims are able to so casually label non-Muslims as dogs and swine. For example, His Eminence the Grand Ayatollah Al-Sayyid Ali Al-Sistani, in his *Islamic Laws,* "Najis Things: *Kafir,*" classifies the *kafir* (non-Muslim infidel) as *najis* (dirty, impure, unclean), on the same level as dogs and pigs.[7]

If such labeling is offensive to Dr. Baagil, he need not take any offense from Jesus, who never called the Gentiles (or any person) dogs or swine. His words at Matthew 7:6 are "Do not give what is holy to the dogs; nor cast your pearls before swine." Jesus is teaching by analogy, stating that teaching should be given in line with the spiritual capacity of the student. Nowhere does He suggest that the Gentiles are dogs or swine. Rather, He openly gives His teaching, the greatest of pearls, to Gentiles, and even heals a Gentile woman's daughter (Mark 7:24-30) and transformed a Samaritan woman's life (John 4:7-30).

(b) "Woman, what does your concern have to do with Me?"

When the wedding at Cana ran out of wine, Mary came to Jesus and told him, "They have no wine" (John 2:3). Before performing His first miracle of turning water into wine, Jesus said to her, "Woman, what does your concern have to do with Me?" (John 2:4).

Dr. Baagil interprets Jesus' addressing His mother as "woman" as insolence not befitting of a prophet. Yet such a conclusion is unsupported. In English, "woman" and "man" are sometimes used to address people, and they are not always disrespectful. Yet even if they were disrespectful titles in English, such tone should not be imputed to the language spoken by Jesus. The connotations of respect and disrespect of a word in a given language are subtle and the tone of a word will vary in different languages and even sometimes in the same language. For example, "lady" essentially means the same thing as "woman," but in modern America, to address a woman as "lady" may have a slightly condescending tone (e.g., "listen, lady"), but in England, implies nobility (e.g., "Lady Victoria").

The original Greek for "woman" used in John 2:4 is γυνή (*gynē,* G1135). It appears 221 times in 200 verses of the New Testament, including:

- Mat 15:28: Jesus answered and said to the Gentile woman whose daughter was ill, 'O woman, great is your faith!'" In His

---

[7] *Islamic Laws*, available at <http://www.sistani.org/english/book/48/2132>.

praise of the woman, His use of the word "woman" is not insolent.

- Luke 13:12: Jesus saw a woman with an infirmity who was bent over and called her and said, "Woman, you are loosed from your infirmity." Jesus' act is one of compassion. The use of "woman" is not intended to be disrespectful.
- John 20:13, 15: The angels and Jesus said to Mary Magdalene, "Woman, why are you weeping?" Here, the angels and Jesus approach Mary Magdalene with compassion, not with contempt or ridicule.
- Col 3:19: Paul commands husbands to "love your wives and do not be bitter toward them." The Greek γυνή is here translated in the NKJV as "wives," but it is the same as the word translated as "woman" in John 2:4, except that Paul employs the plural of the term. Paul is commanding husbands to "love" their wives (women). There is nothing here condescending about the reference to women. Rather, it is just the opposite, as Paul is commanding that they be treated with love.
- 1Pe 3:1: Peter states that husbands "may be won by the conduct of their wives." The original Greek for "wives" is again γυνή (woman), except that it is in the plural. Peter indicates how through women, husbands can be won over. Peter points to the potential of women in winning salvation. Addressing them as "women" is not in any way insolent.

12. The Old Testament "Prophecies" of Revelation to Be Given in Arabic to One Who Is Illiterate

Dr. Baagil's final argument is that the Old Testament prophecies that a revelation will be given in Arabic to one who is illiterate, *i.e.*, Muhammad. He divides his argument into two parts: (i) Isaiah prophecies a revelation to one who is illiterate; and (ii) Zephania prophecies that the revelation will be in Arabic. We will deal with each argument in turn.

a. Revelation to One who is Illiterate

Isaiah writes that "the book is delivered to one who is illiterate, saying, 'Read this, please.' And he says, 'I am not literate'" (Isa 29:12). Dr. Baagil believes that this prophecy is fulfilled in Muhammad, as the "first revelation of *Allah* through the angel Gabriel to Muhammad [PBUH] was the word '*Iqra*' which means 'Read' (rehearse) in *Surah* 96:1-5. As [Muhammad] was illiterate he replied: 'I cannot read'" (p. 69).

There are several problems in Dr. Baagil's argument:

i.   *Surah* 96:1 Commands Muhammad not to "Read," but to "Recite"

Surah 96:1-5 does not indicate that Muhammad was told to read. Although the Maulana Muhammad Ali Translation renders 96:1 as "read," it would more accurately be translated as "confess" or "recite." The original language used is not the Arabic اقْرَأ ("read") on its own, but rather, the Arabic اقْرَأ بِ, which, with the additional preposition بِ, translates as "confess," "acknowledge" or, as traditionally understood by Muslims, "recite." Therefore, the text of *Surah* 96:1, which commands Muhammad to "recite," has no relationship with Isaiah 29:12, which commands an illiterate man to "read."

ii. Accepting Dr. Baagil's Flawed Translation of *Surah* 96:1 Renders Illogical Results

If we were to accept Dr. Baagil's incorrect translation of *Surah* 96:1 as "read," the verse would be rendered illogical. According to Islamic tradition, the *Qur'an* was written by scribes who recorded Muhammad's words as he recited that which was given to him by the angel Gabriel. If the angel Gabriel, upon first appearing to Muhammad, commanded him to "read," then what was Muhammad given to read? There was no *Qur'an* written at the time, as Muhammad had not yet recited it. This illogical conclusion can only be explained if we read the entire phrase اقْرَأ بِ, which includes the preposition بِ, which renders the meaning as "confess," "acknowledge" or "recite" in English.

Yet even if we accept Dr. Baagil's flawed rendition of *Surah* 96:1, then any person can claim to prophesy in God's name and then assert authenticity on the basis of his or her illiteracy. On this basis, the prophecies of the apostles, who were also unlearned and uneducated (Acts 4:13), are just as valid.

Moreover, if indeed *Surah* 96:1 commands Muhammad to "read," and he does in fact reply "I cannot read" (p. 69), then according to Islamic tradition, he ultimate does "read" because the angel catches hold of him, at which time the first verses of the *Qur'an* are "read" (recited). Isaiah 29:12, in contrast, never indicates that the one who is illiterate reads.

b. The Revelation will be in Arabic

i. Dr. Baagil's Argument

Next, Dr. Baagil argues that the Isaiah 29:12 prophecy that would be delivered to one who is not "learned" will be given in Arabic on the basis of the following verses:

- Isaiah 28:11: "For with stammering lips and *another tongue* He will speak to this people."
- Zephania 3:9: "For then I will restore to the peoples a *pure language*, That they all may call on the name of the Lord, To serve Him with one accord."

Dr. Baagil argues that "another tongue" and "pure language" is Arabic, the language of Muhammad's revelation. He writes that "[a]nother tongue means here another language, not Hebrew or Aramaic but Arabic" (p. 69) and that the "unity" of the language prophesied by Zephania is Arabic because "Muslims all over the world are using one language, which is Arabic, in calling their God, in their prayers, pilgrimage and in their greetings to each other ... Alas the Truth has come in Arabic" (p. 69).

ii. Problems in Dr. Baagil's Argument

Dr. Baagil's argument is flawed in the following respects:

(1) Dr. Baagil Randomly Picks Arabic as the "Other Language," Yet It Could Just as Easily Apply to Aramaic or Other Languages

Dr. Baagil argues that "another tongue" in Isaiah means "another language, not Hebrew or Aramaic but Arabic" (p. 69), but gives no support whatsoever for his conclusion. While it may be logical that the "other language" would be distinct from Hebrew, the language in which Isaiah wrote his prophecy, he gives no reason whatsoever as to why the other language would not be Aramaic, the language Jesus spoke, which is distinct from Hebrew, or any of the many languages that later men who claimed to be prophets would use. For example, Joseph Smith could argue that the "other language" is actually English, the language used in the revelation of the Book of Mormon.

(2) The True Meaning of Isaiah 28:10-11: The "Tongue" of Judgment and the Gift of Tongues

As is customary, Dr. Baagil quotes a verse without citing its context. Isaiah 28:11 falls within a series of verses in which Isaiah warns Ephraim, one of the northern tribes of Israel, of God's imminent judgment (*see* Isa 28:1, 3). Isaiah 28:9 indicates that the audience of Isaiah's message was not ready to receive it, for they are like those "just weaned from milk" and "just drawn from the breasts." The verse that follows, Isaiah 28:10, is gibberish in the original Hebrew, though it is written to rhyme. This indicates that to Isaiah's audience, the message he preached, rather than being heeded, was taken as gibberish.

God calls Ephraim to "rest" and "refreshing ... Yet they would not hear" (Isa 28:12). Therefore, the word of the LORD was to them like gibberish, "Precept upon precept, precept upon precept, Line upon line, line upon line, Here a little, there a little" such that they would "go and fall backward, and be broken and snared and caught" (Isa 28:13), ultimately by the Assyrians.

It is within this context that Isaiah declares that "with stammering lips and another tongue He will speak to this people" (Isa 28:11). There are various ways of translating the original Hebrew: The NKJV uses for "stammering lips" and "another tongue"; the NIV uses "foreign lips" and "strange tongues." The point here is that, because Ephraim refused to heed Isaiah's warning, God would speak through them through another tongue—the tongue of the Assyrians, who would conquer and bring about God's judgment on Israel.

At the same time, the "strange tongues" that God would use to speak to His people are referenced by the Apostle Paul in his First Letter to the Corinthians. Quoting Isaiah 28:11-12, Paul writes, "In the law it is written: 'With men of other tongues and other lips I will speak to this people; and yet, for all that, they will not hear Me,' says the Lord. Therefore tongues are for a sign, not to those who believe but to unbelievers" (1Co 14:21-22). The Isaiah 28:11 "other language" is therefore not Arabic, as Dr. Baagil asserts, but rather the gift of tongues given as a gift of the Holy Spirit, given as a sign for unbelievers. God therefore speaks through the "tongue" of judgment in the Old Testament and through the New Testament gift of tongues in the New Testament.

(3) The True Meaning of Zephania 3:9: The Restoration of "Pure" Language

Dr. Baagil argues that the "unity" of the language prophesied by Zephania is Arabic because "Muslims all over the world are using one language, which is Arabic, in calling their God, in their prayers, pilgrimage and in their greetings to each other … Alas the Truth has come in Arabic" (p. 69). But Zephania does not prophesy about the "unity" of language. Rather, he prophesies about a "pure" language. Zephania writes that God will "restore to the peoples a pure language, That they all may call on the name of the Lord, To serve Him with one accord" (Zep 3:9).

There are various translations of Zephania 3:9, which make it clear that God is not speaking about raising up a prophet who speaks a particular language, but rather, about a purification of the words spoken of a people, which is to be a reflection of a general purification. The NIV translates Zephania 3:9 as "I will purify the lips of the peoples, that all of them may call on the name of the Lord." By this, the prophet means that God will remove the evil on the people's lips and replace it with pure language that can be used to "call on the name of the Lord" (Zep 3:9). That this verse is a general announcement of the redemption of the Lord, rather than bringing forth a prophet who will bring about a new prophet speaking a different language, is made clear by the verses following Zephania 3:9: "In that day you shall not be shamed for any of your deeds In which you transgress against Me … you shall no longer be haughty In My holy mountain" (Zep 3:11); "The remnant of Israel shall do no unrighteousness and speak no lies, Nor shall a deceitful tongue be found in their mouth" (Zep 3:13).

CHAPTER 3. COULD MAN CORRUPT THE REVELATIONS OF GOD AND OTHER HARD QUESTIONS

I. Could Man Corrupt the Revelations of Almighty God?

What is remarkable about the argument about biblical corruption is that it concedes that, although God is omnipotent, man was able to corrupt a line of nearly forty prophets, from Abraham to Moses to Joshua to Ezra to Nehemiah to Solomon to David to Isaiah to Ezekiel to Daniel to Hosea to Joel to Micah to Haggai to Zechariah to Malachi, all of whom, according to Islam, originally preached that Ishmael was the son of promise, that there was no God but *Allah*, and that prophesied the coming of Muhammad. Man was able not only to change this message to teach that Isaac was the son of promise and that God had raised up prophets in his line and to put forth countless prophecies of the life of Jesus and salvation through Him, but also, man was able to obliterate all traces of the original Islamic texts, all except for the Gospel of Barnabas, which does prophecy the coming of Muhammad, but which scholars overwhelmingly agree is a fifteen or sixteenth century forgery.

What this means is that, if man is able to corrupt God's Revelation to Moses, David, Jesus and other prophets, then clearly man is capable of corrupting God's Revelation to Muhammad. No reason is given whereby earlier revelation is more vulnerable to corruption than Muhammad's revelation, or why Muhammad's revelation is immune from corruption.

II. Why Would God Make a Covenant with Ishmael and then Send All of the Prophets (Except Muhammad) through Isaac?

Dr. Baagil argues that Ishmael, not Isaac, was the son of God's covenant with Abraham and that God commanded Abraham to sacrifice Ishmael, not Isaac: "the Islamic version states that the covenant between God, Abraham and his only son Ishmael was made and sealed when Ishmael was supposed to be sacrificed. And on the same day were Abraham, Ishmael and all men of the household circumcised while Isaac was not even born yet" (p. 52). "The descendants of Ishmael, Prophet Muhammad [PBUT], including all Muslims, remain faithful until today to this covenant of circumcision" (p. 53).

These allegations raise some very important questions:

- First, why would God choose Ishmael as the promised son of the covenant, but then raise up all of the prophets through Isaac? Muslims do not deny that all of the biblical prophets, from Joseph to Moses, Elijah, Elisha, Isaiah, Daniel, Jeremiah, Ezekiel, Hosea, Joel, Amos, Jonah, Zechariah, John the Baptist and Jesus are all the offspring of Isaac through his son Jacob ("Israel"). In addition, the kings that the Muslims regard as prophets, including Saul, David and Solomon, as well as other Hebrew figures that Muslims consider to be prophets, such as Lot, Samson and Nehemiah, are all also descendants of Isaac through Jacob ("Israel"). For the Muslim, the dozens of prophets that God raised up were thus the descendants of Isaac, and Ishmael's line was barren of any prophecy until the seventh century (assuming that Muhammad, whose message contradicted that of all of the prophets that preceded him, could even be considered a prophet)?

- If God sent Ishmael and Hagar to establish a new settlement in Mecca, and through Ishmael He intended to establish His covenant, then what Scriptures did Ishmael and his descendants use from the time they were separated from Abraham until the time that Muhammad appeared? Since they were separated from the Israelites, they would not have had access to the Israel's Scriptures. Therefore, these "true Muslims" would have been without any of the prophecies, beginning first with Moses and then concluding with Jesus.

CHAPTER 4. RESPONSE TO ISLAM'S POLITICAL CLAIMS

I. Inequality between the Races: A Response to Malcolm X

A. Overview

According to Ghada Khafagy's tract "Where Hearts and Souls Meet,"[8] Hajj is a life-changing experience for many pilgrims. Malcolm X, the African American Muslim activist, came back from Makkah with totally different convictions. "Hajj had a profound effect on his perspective on race and racism," she writes. Malcolm X wrote in one of his letters[9]:

> There were tens of thousands of pilgrims, from all over the world. They were of all colors, from blue-eyed blondes to black-skinned Africans. But we were all participating in the same ritual, displaying a spirit of unity and brotherhood that my experiences in America had led me to believe never could exist between the white and non-white.

B. Problems in Malcolm X's Account

There are multiple errors in Ms. Khafagy's account, a few of which we point out herein:

- It is most unfortunate that Ms. Khafagy points to a radical Muslim who advocated the use of violence as an agent of social change as an example of a man "changed" by *Hajj*. He is famous for having declared his objective for equality "by any means necessary," which, of course, includes violence, and for criticizing Dr. Martin Luther King, Jr.'s non-violent approach and contrasting it with his own approach.[10] Although Malcolm

---

[8] Available at
<http://ascertainthetruth.com/att/index.php?option=com_content&view=article&id=377:where-hearts-a-souls-meet&catid=64:understanding-al-islam&Itemid=53>.
[9] Available at
<http://ascertainthetruth.com/att/index.php?option=com_content&view=article&id=377:where-hearts-a-souls-meet&catid=64:understanding-al-islam&Itemid=53>.
[10] For example, the following quote has been attributed to Malcolm X: "The goal has

X conceded that he would prefer, where possible, non-violence means of social change, he conceded that "when you drop that violence on me, then you've made me go insane, and I'm not responsible for what I do."[11] Many readers will be left asking whether it was *Hajj* and other rituals, practices and beliefs ancillary to Islam that may have inspired Malcolm X's advocacy of violence.

-    Malcolm X's participation in *Hajj* may have been marked by thousands of pilgrims of diverse ethnicities and nationalities coming together in harmony, but this has not always been the case. Countless *Hajj* tragedies have left Muslims of different nations and sects pointing fingers over one another for who is responsible for the deaths of hundreds or even thousands of Muslims. The most recent example is the 2015 *Hajj* stampede, which left at least 1,399 killed,[12] with Indonesia[13] and Iran[14] criticizing or blaming Saudi Arabia for the tragedy. The tragedy fueled further tensions between Sunni Saudi Arabia and Shiites in Lebanon and Iran,[15] and was certainly not the first one to do so.

-    Yet even if in *Hajj*, Muslims from all over the world came together in peace and harmony, this has little relevance for the broader question of whether *Hajj* and Islam more broadly promote harmony among Muslims. Of course, one need look no further than the daily headlines or any standard history of Islam to find perennial fighting between the various sects of Islam. Today, Shia Houthis embattle a Sunni regime in Yemen;

---

always been the same, with the approaches to it as different as mine and Dr. Martin Luther King's non-violent marching, that dramatizes the brutality and the evil of the white man against defenseless blacks. And in the racial climate of this country today, it is anybody's guess which of the 'extremes' in approach to the black man's problems might personally meet a fatal catastrophe first – 'non-violent' Dr. King, or so-called 'violent' me." *See* <http://www.malcolm-x.org/quotes.htm>.

[11] *Id.*

[12] *See* <http://www.todayszaman.com/anasayfa_new-tally-in-saudi-hajj-disaster-shows-at-least-1399-killed_401022.html>.

[13] *See* < http://www.japantimes.co.jp/news/2015/09/29/world/indonesia-criticizes-saudi-arabia-hajj-disaster-response/#.VoTJdnTfqn4>.

[14] *See* < http://www.theguardian.com/world/2015/sep/25/iran-blames-saudi-government-hajj-disaster-investigation>.

[15] *See* <http://www.ibtimes.com/high-death-toll-hajj-stampede-fuels-further-tensions-between-sunni-saudi-arabia-2129588>.

Sunni Islamists in Syria wage war against a government dominated by Alawis; Sunni ISIS in Iraq battles Kurds who are mostly Sunni and Shia militias; the list goes on.

- For all of their problems and imperfections, race relations in the United States are far better than they are in most Muslim nations. While America abolished slavery in 1865, slavery continued in many Muslim nations right up into recent times, having been abolished in Saudi Arabia and Yemen in 1962, in the United Arab Emirates in 1964 and in Oman in 1970. Today, though it was made a crime in 2007, slavery exists *de jure* in Mauritania.[16] Other problems persist in race relations is Islamic countries, including mistreatment of foreign domestic workers, reported in various human rights reports.

- One need look no further than the relations between the Arab countries themselves to find the opposite of what Malcolm X calls "unity." Everywhere, the Arab nations close off their borders to one another and discriminate against citizens of other Arab nations while courting Westerners and other non-Arabs. For example, a national of most Western nations can enter Erbil and other cities in Iraqi Kurdistan without obtaining a visa; nationals of Arab countries, in contrast, must go through a rigorous visa process. Nationals of many Western nations can obtain visit visas to Saudi Arabia with validity of two years and, in the cast of American nationals, five years. Most Arabs are unable to get visas with validity of more than 90 days. Other examples abound.

---

[16] "Slavery's last stronghold," available at
<http://edition.cnn.com/interactive/2012/03/world/mauritania.slaverys.last.stronghold>.

CHAPTER 5. THE PURPOSE OF CREATION

I. Introduction

The Purpose of Creation is a book written by Dr. Bilal Philips that argues that man was created to submit to *Allāh* and spread the message of Islam. In addition, he argues that God created man so that man would worship and remember God. He states that the Christian explanation of the purpose of creation—the recognition of the "divine sacrifice" of Jesus Christ—is inadequate because Christ was not a man of all time; only those who lived at the time of Christ or after Christ could partake in this purpose. In this section of this book, all page references refer to Dr. Philips' treatise.

Dr. Philips' theses are flawed on several levels. First, he fails to understand that the divine sacrifice offered by Christ is not the Christian purpose of creation. Rather, it is the way to salvation offered by God. The Christian purpose of creation is not unlike the purpose that Dr. Philips describes in his book. God created creation for His glory and man was created to worship God: "in order that we, who were the first to put our hope in Christ, might be for the praise of his glory" (Eph 1:12). In the same way, God's redemption of those who are in his "possession" is "to the praise of his glory" (Eph 1:14).

To the extent that Dr. Philips recognizes that man was created to worship God, he is correct. However, we do not need Islam to teach this; it has been taught for millennia in the Judeo-Christian tradition. At the same time, however, Dr. Philips makes certain assertions as to Christian doctrine (*e.g.*, salvation through Christ excludes those who lived before Christ) that are inaccurate or patently false. This book refutes such claims and sets forth true Christian doctrine.

II. Individual Claims and Replies

A. The Christian Purpose of Creation Is the "Recognition of the 'Divine Sacrifice'"

1. Claim

Dr. Philips claims that the Christian purpose of creation is to recognize that Jesus is the son of God and the only way to eternal life. He writes (p. 9-10):

> [T]he Christian purpose of creation became the recognition of the 'divine sacrifice' and the acceptance of Jesus Christ as the Lord God. This may be deduced from the following words attributed to Jesus in the Gospel according to John, "For God so loved the world that he gave his only Son, that whoever believes in him should not perish but have eternal life."

2. Response: Faith in Jesus is the Way to Salvation, not the Purpose of Creation

Dr. Philips is mistaken in characterizing the recognition of Jesus as the Son of God as the purpose of creation. Recognizing Jesus as the Son of God is not the purpose of creation; it is the door to eternal life. This is made clear in John 3:16:

> For God so loved the world that He gave His only begotten Son, that whoever believes in Him should not perish but have everlasting life.

B. Salvation through Christ Excludes All of the People Who Lived Before Christ

1. Claim

Dr. Philips claims that the Christian purpose of creation is to recognize that Jesus is the son of God and the only way to eternal life. He writes (p. 9-10):

> [T]he Christian purpose of creation became the recognition of the 'divine sacrifice' and the acceptance of Jesus Christ as the Lord God. This may be deduced from the following words attributed to Jesus in the Gospel according to John, "For God so loved the world that he gave his only Son, that whoever believes in him should not perish but have eternal life." However, if this is the purpose of creation and the prerequisite for everlasting life, why was it not taught by all the prophets? Why did God not become man in the time of Adam and his offspring so that all mankind would have an equal chance to fulfill their purpose for existence and attain everlasting life.

Regarding the purpose of creation, Dr. Philips impugns the biblical message of faith in Jesus and implies that it is inherently unjust because it means that only those who had a chance to hear about Jesus, not those who lived before Jesus or those who lived after Him but never heard the Gospel, have a chance to be saved. His argument is flawed on several levels.

2.   Response 1: All Have Knowledge and Are Without Excuse

a.   *The Gospel Is Preached to All People, Who Are Without Excuse*

i.   The Gospel Will Be Preached in "All the World" (Mat 24:14)

Jesus stated that the Gospel will be preached "in all the world":

> Mat 24:14 And this gospel of the kingdom will be preached in all the world as a witness to all the nations, and then the end will come.

ii.   The Gospel Was Preached to Even the Dead (1Pe 3:19, 1Pe 4:6)

(1)   The "Spirits in Prison" (1Pe 3:19)

Christ preached to the "spirits in prison" (1Pe 3:19):

> 1Pe 3:18 For Christ also suffered once for sins, the just for the unjust, that He might bring us to God, being put to death in the flesh but made alive by the Spirit,
> 1Pe 3:19 by whom also He went and preached to the spirits in prison,
> 1Pe 3:20 who formerly were disobedient, when once the Divine longsuffering waited in the days of Noah, while the ark was being prepared, in which a few, that is, eight souls, were saved through water.

An imprisoned "spirit" can only logically be understood to mean a person who is dead. If Peter is saying in 3:18 that Jesus was raised from the dead by the power of the Spirit, then he's saying at the beginning of 3:19 that "by [the Spirit] also [Jesus] went and preached to the spirits in prison." Many interpreters have taken Peter to be saying that between Jesus's death and the resurrection or possibly after the resurrection, Jesus preached the Gospel to the dead who "formerly were disobedient" (1Pe 3:20).

(2)   The Gospel was Preached to the Dead (1Pe 4:6)

Peter writes:

> 1Pe 4:4 In regard to these, they think it strange that you do not run with them in the same flood of dissipation, speaking evil of you.

1Pe 4:5 They will give an account to Him who is ready to judge the living and the dead.

1Pe 4:6 For this reason the gospel was preached also to those who are dead, that they might be judged according to men in the flesh, but live according to God in the spirit.

1 Peter 4:6 does not specify whether the Gospel was preached to those who are dead while they were living or after they died. This has been a subject of speculation and debate among scholars, but the view that the gospel was preached to the dead after they died holds textual support. David G. Horell writes[17]:

> The interpretation of 1 Pet 4.6 which sees 'the dead' as Christians who heard the gospel during their lifetime but who have since died is becoming increasingly widely accepted, especially in recent commentaries in English. William Dalton's monograph Christ's Proclamation to the Spirits has been influential in promoting this view. However, despite its current popularity, there are serious problems with this interpretation, especially in its dependence on assuming a primitive eschatological context for 1 Peter. The view of the verse as referring to a proclamation made to people already dead, on the other hand, is more plausible than recent commentators suggest, and can be defended against their criticisms.

iii. God's Invisible Attributes and Nature Are Seen through Creation; We Are Without Excuse (Rom 1:18-21)

God's invisible attributes, eternal power and Godhead are seen through the creation. Therefore, we are without excuse:

> Rom 1:18 For the wrath of God is revealed from heaven against all ungodliness and unrighteousness of men, who suppress the truth in unrighteousness,
>
> Rom 1:19 because what may be known of God is manifest in them, for God has shown it to them.

---

[17] David G. Horell, "Who are 'The Dead' and When was the Gospel Preached to Them?: The Interpretation of 1 Pet 4.6," *New Testament Studies*, Cambridge University Press (Volume 49, Issue 1, Jan. 2003), available at <https://www.cambridge.org/core/journals/new-testament-studies/article/who-are-the-dead-and-when-was-the-gospel-preached-to-them-the-interpretation-of-1-pet-46/66D1EF6323D7CD9AEEA78CF9AF8309AF>.

> Rom 1:20 For since the creation of the world His invisible attributes are clearly seen, being understood by the things that are made, *even His eternal power and Godhead*, so that they are *without excuse*,
> Rom 1:21 because, although they knew God, they did not glorify Him as God, nor were thankful, but became futile in their thoughts, and their foolish hearts were darkened.
> …

As the book of Romans makes clear, it is not necessary to be a Christian or a Jew in order to have knowledge of God's law. God's law is written into our hearts (Rom 1:20).

iv. The law is Written on the Hearts of the Gentiles (Rom 2:14-16)

Paul's letter to the Romans addresses the issue of those who never heard of Jesus and do not have the law, and yet know God's law because it is "written on their hearts" (Rom 2:15). He writes:

> Rom 2:14 for when Gentiles, who do not have the law, by nature do the things in the law, these, although not having the law, are a law to themselves,
> Rom 2:15 who show the work of the law written in their hearts, their conscience also bearing witness, and between themselves their thoughts accusing or else excusing them)
> Rom 2:16 in the day when God will judge the secrets of men by Jesus Christ, according to my gospel.

v. Therefore, We Are Without Excuse (Rom 1:20)

As Paul states, we are without excuse (Rom 1:20). This is because God's eternal power and nature are known to all and also because they are preached to all. As Jesus said in Matthew 24:14, the "gospel of the kingdom will be preached in all the world." The Bible indicates that the Gospel was preached to even those who died without hearing the Gospel—*i.e.*, the "spirits in prison" (1Pe 3:19) and to the dead (1Pe 4:6).

b. Salvation was Always Offered through Covenant, Even in the Old Testament

i. Overview

Under the New Covenant, No one comes to the Father except through Jesus (John 14:6). However, it is inaccurate to characterize the

New Covenant ushered in by Jesus as a means to salvation that was not available to those who preceded Jesus. Even in the pre-Christ era, Gentiles could come to salvation by covenant. Since the fall of Adam and Eve, "all have sinned and fall short of the glory of God" (Rom 3:23). But this does not mean that all have perished. Disobedience has always been the means to separation from God and the pathway to death, whereas faith in God has always been the means of salvation. God entered into various Covenants with mankind since the days of Creation that manifested the relationship between obedience and sin to salvation and death:

- God entered into a covenant with Adam based on the condition of obedience. The result of Adam's disobedience was physical death and the corruption of creation (*see* Gen 3:19).
- God entered into a covenant with Noah whereby God promised that he would never again send another flood to destroy creation, as he did with Noah's flood to wipe out corruption and wickedness from the face of the earth (*see* Gen 9:12-17).
- Abraham's Covenant with God is found in Genesis 12:1-3:

  Gen 12:1 Now the Lord had said to Abram: "Get out of your country, from your family And from your father's house, To a land that I will show you.
  Gen 12:2 I will make you a great nation; I will bless you and make your name great; And you shall be a blessing.
  Gen 12:3 I will bless those who bless you, And I will curse him who curses you; And in you all the families of the earth shall be blessed."

- Moses' Covenant with God is recorded in the Pentateuch. God established a Covenant with the Israelites when He saved them from slavery in Egypt into the promised land of Canaan.

ii. Instances in the Old Testament Where God's Word Is Preached to Gentiles

In the book of Jonah, God called Jonah, an Israelite, to go to Nineveh, the capital of the Assyrian Empire, to warn it of its destruction because of its sins. Jonah refused to accept his divine mission and left on a sea voyage instead. After being swallowed by a fish, Jonah was given a second chance to send a warning to Nineveh. This time, he carried out the commission.

Because of the universality of God's love shown in the book, it has been called a counterpart of John 3:16. It demonstrates that God's message of repentance was never limited to the Israelites. Rather, God is "not willing that any should perish but that all should come to repentance" (2Pe 3:9).

iii. Throughout the Old Testament, Gentiles Came to Believe in the Lord

Gentiles were grafted into Israel through conversions recounted throughout the Old Testament. Examples of conversions include Abram, Moses' father-in-law Jethro, Naaman the commander of the Syrian Army and leper, Ruth the Moabite, Rahab the harlot and the sailors on board the ship with Jonah, and the Ninevites.

iv. God Spoke through Non-Israelite Prophets

The Old Testament also makes clear that God used non-Israelites as prophet through whom He spoke. An example of this is Balaam.

v. Israel Was Chosen to be a Kingdom of Priests to All Nations

The Scriptures make clear that God chosen Israel to be a priesthood to all nations:

> Isa 61:6 But you shall be named the priests of the Lord, They shall call you the servants of our God. You shall eat the riches of the Gentiles, And in their glory you shall boast.
> Exo 19:6 And you shall be to Me a kingdom of priests and a holy nation.'

A priest is someone who spiritually ministers to others. A "kingdom of priests" is a kingdom, all of whose members are commissioned to spiritually minister to other kingdoms of peoples. By designating Israel as a "kingdom of priests," God identified Israel as His chosen people to receive His word and spread it to other nations.

In many ways, Israel fell short of God's commandment to be priests to other nations. Even Jonah, a prophet commissioned by God to preach repentance to the Ninevites, rebelled against God and tried to flee from Him. God eventually opened up the floodgates of salvation through His Son Jesus Christ. God's chosen priesthood was no longer based on the bloodline of Israel. Rather, Gentiles were grafted into the kingdom through faith in Christ. In this way, Peter writes:

1Pe 2:9 But you are a chosen generation, a royal priesthood, a holy nation, His own special people, that you may proclaim the praises of Him who called you out of darkness into His marvelous light;

vi. Faith was the Means of Justification Even in the Old Testament

Paul makes clear in the book of Romans that faith was always the means to righteousness and salvation, including in the Old Testament covenants:

> Rom 4:2 For if Abraham was justified by works, he has something to boast about, but not before God.
> Rom 4:3 For what does the Scripture say? "ABRAHAM BELIEVED GOD, AND IT WAS ACCOUNTED TO HIM FOR RIGHTEOUSNESS."
> Rom 4:4 Now to him who works, the wages are not counted as grace but as debt.
> Rom 4:5 But to him who does not work but believes on Him who justifies the ungodly, his faith is accounted for righteousness,
> Rom 4:6 just as David also describes the blessedness of the man to whom God imputes righteousness apart from works:
> Rom 4:7 "BLESSED ARE THOSE WHOSE LAWLESS DEEDS ARE FORGIVEN, AND WHOSE SINS ARE COVERED;
> Rom 4:8 BLESSED IS THE MAN TO WHOM THE LORD SHALL NOT IMPUTE SIN."
> Rom 4:9 Does this blessedness then come upon the circumcised only, or upon the uncircumcised also? For we say that faith was accounted to Abraham for righteousness.
> Rom 4:10 How then was it accounted? While he was circumcised, or uncircumcised? Not while circumcised, but while uncircumcised.
> Rom 4:11 And he received the sign of circumcision, a seal of the righteousness of the faith which he had while still uncircumcised, that he might be the father of all those who believe, though they are uncircumcised, that righteousness might be imputed to them also,
> Rom 4:12 and the father of circumcision to those who not only are of the circumcision, but who also walk in the steps of the faith which our father Abraham had while still uncircumcised.
> Rom 4:13 For the promise that he would be the heir of the world was not to Abraham or to his seed through the law, but through the righteousness of faith.
> ...
> Rom 4:22 And therefore "IT WAS ACCOUNTED TO HIM FOR RIGHTEOUSNESS."

Rom 4:23 Now it was not written for his sake alone that it was imputed to him,
Rom 4:24 but also for us. It shall be imputed to us who believe in Him who raised up Jesus our Lord from the dead,
Rom 4:25 who was delivered up because of our offenses, and was raised because of our justification.

The law has always been the means of convicting us of sin, whereas faith was always been the means to salvation. Mankind has never earned salvation through works. "All have sinned and fall short of the glory of God" (Rom 3:23). Throughout the Old Testament, the Israelites offered sacrifices to God as sin coverings. God fulfilled the Old Testament law of sacrificial atonement by sending Jesus, the final sacrificial lamb. Hebrews 9:11-12 proclaims:

> Christ came as High Priest of the good things to come, with the greater and more perfect tabernacle not made with hands, that is, not of this creation. Not with the blood of goats and calves, but with His own blood He entered the Most Holy Place *once for all, having obtained eternal redemption*.

3. Response 2 : We Are Judged According to What We Know, Not According to What We Do Not Know

a. *Overview*

The Bible supports the idea that people are judged according to what they know, not according to what they do not know. Jesus said that "God so loved the world that He gave His only begotten Son, that whoever believes in Him should not perish but have everlasting life" (John 3:16), but he did not say that a person had to have knowledge of and faith in the resurrection in order to be saved. Such a proposition would mean that all of those who came before Jesus and had no knowledge of Him or of the resurrection would perish. Rather, Jesus says that those who believe in Jesus would have everlasting life. Belief in Jesus should be read as belief in God, since Jesus was God (*see, e.g.*, John 10:30, "I and My Father are one").

b. *The Example of Abraham Is Instructive*

God met Abram and revealed to him that he would have an heir from his own body (Gen 15:4). God told Abram to "Look now toward heaven, and count the stars if you are able to number them ... So shall your descendants be" (Gen 15:5). Abram "believed in the Lord, and He accounted it to him for righteousness" (Gen 15:6).

Abram was counted as righteous not because of faith in Christ and the resurrection, of which he had no knowledge, but because of his faith in the promise that God revealed to him. As a result of Abram's faith, he did not perish. Rather, he was taken to a place of "comfort" in the afterlife, a place on the other side of a deep chasm from Hades and its torments (see Luke 16:22-26). He got there through faith in the message that God had revealed to him, not through faith in a message that had not yet been revealed.

c. Jesus Taught that We Are Accountable for What We Know

This is consistent with Jesus' teaching about those who innocently reject him. Jesus said: "If I had not come and spoken to them, they would have no sin, but now they have no excuse for their sin" (John 15:22). Once a person comes to know the truth, he must embrace it or he will be culpable of rejecting it. We see this in Jesus' words to the Pharisees: "If you were blind, you would have no guilt; but now that you say, 'We see,' your guilt remains" (John 9:41).

d. The Catechism of the Catholic Church Teaches that We Are Accountable for What We Know

The Catechism of the Catholic Church teaches:

> Every man who is ignorant of the gospel of Christ and of his Church but seeks the truth and does the will of God in accordance with his understanding of it can be saved. It may be supposed that such persons would have desired baptism explicitly if they had known its necessity (CCC 1260).

The Catechism clarifies:

> This affirmation is not aimed at those who, through no fault of their own, do not know Christ and his Church: "Those who, through no fault of their own, do not know the Gospel of Christ or his Church, but who nevertheless seek God with a sincere heart, and, moved by grace, try in their actions to do his will as they know it through the dictates of their conscience – those too may achieve eternal salvation" (quoting, Lumen Gentium, 16).

It is not ignorance that enables salvation; ignorance excuses only lack of knowledge. That which opens the salvation to those who do not know Christ is their conscious effort, under grace, to serve God as well as they can on the basis of the best information they have about him.

The Church speaks of "implicit desire" or "longing" that can exist in the hearts of those who seek God but are ignorant of the means of his grace. If a person longs for salvation but does not know the divinely established means of salvation, he is said to have an implicit desire for membership in the Church.

e. Sacrifice was the Means of Covering for Sin Even before Christ's Time

Dr. Philips' suggestion that Jesus introduced a new or different way into a relationship with God is incorrect. It is actually a continuation of the Old Covenant. In the Old Covenant, covering for sin was given through atonement sacrifice and offering. Jesus offered those in the New Covenant a final sacrificial offering and covering for sin once and for all (Heb 10:10).

4. Response 3: God Calls Us to Spread the Gospel

The emphasis given in the Gospels, the Book of Acts and the Epistles on spreading the Gospel demonstrates the fact that knowledge of Christ and the Gospel is the mechanism that God chose for the salvation of the world. Because salvation can only come through this knowledge, God enjoins all Christians to be His witnesses through spreading the Gospel.

a. Salvation Requires Calling on the Lord, Which Requires Belief, Which Requires Hearing the Gospel, Which Requires Preaching the Gospel (Rom 10:13-15)

Paul writes that Christians must be sent to spread the Gospel of salvation:

> Rom 10:9 that if you confess with your mouth the Lord Jesus and believe in your heart that God has raised Him from the dead, you will be saved.
>
> ...
>
> Rom 10:13 For "WHOEVER CALLS ON THE NAME OF THE Lord SHALL BE SAVED."

Rom 10:14 How then shall they call on Him in whom they have not believed? And how shall they believe in Him of whom they have not heard? And how shall they hear without a preacher?

Rom 10:15 And how shall they preach unless they are sent?

b. *Make Disciples of All Nations (Mat 28:19; Mark 16:15)*

Jesus gives His followers the Great Commission in Matthew, commanding His followers to make disciples of all nations:

Mat 28:19 Go therefore and make disciples of all the nations, baptizing them in the name of the Father and of the Son and of the Holy Spirit,

Mark 16 also records the Great Commission. It is rendered as follows;

Mark 16:15 And He said to them, "Go into all the world and preach the gospel to every creature.

c. *The Disciples Will Receive Power to be Witnesses to the End of the Earth (Acts 1:8)*

Jesus promised his followers that He will give them the Holy Spirit to be witnesses to the "end of the earth"[18]:

Acts 1:8 But you shall receive power when the Holy Spirit has come upon you; and you shall be witnesses to Me in Jerusalem, and in all Judea and Samaria, and to the end of the earth."

5. Response 4: Jesus Might Offer Unexpected Ways to Come to the Father

Jesus states, "I am the way, the truth, and the life. No one comes to the Father except through Me" (John 14:6). However, He does not state precisely what "through me" means. He simply states that He is the way to the Father. Jesus could act in unexpected ways to bring those who never heard of Him to the Father.

Luke 23 gives the account of a thief who was crucified next to Jesus. The thief led a sinful life, but he repented and expressed faith in Jesus in the last moments of his life. The thief told the thief crucified on the other side of Jesus that they "receive the due reward of our

---

[18] The NIV translates this verse as "to the ends of the earth."

deeds (Luke 23:41). He then asked Jesus to remember him in Jesus' Kingdom. Jesus then promised that they would be together in paradise:

> Luke 23:42 Then he said to Jesus, "Lord, remember me when You come into Your kingdom."
> Luke 23:43 And Jesus said to him, "Assuredly, I say to you, today you will be with Me in Paradise."

The thief's expression of repentance and faith in Jesus was sufficient to bring him into paradise. If it is possible for a thief who led a sinful life to enter the kingdom of heaven as a result of an expression of faith in the final moments of his life, then it might be possible for Jesus to bring others to the Father, even if they did not live during Jesus' time or if they did not have knowledge of Jesus. It is possible that in the last moments before a person's death, Jesus reveals Himself and offers an opportunity for repentance and a path to salvation.

6.   Dr. Philips' Charge Can Also be Made against Islam

Dr. Philips' charge against Christianity, which is flawed on the bases discussed above, could also be made against Islam. One can argue that it is inherently unjust and unfair that peoples around the world prior to Muhammad were deprived of the opportunity to learn and become aware of God's law because, before God sent Muhammad as a seal of all the prophets, God's message was corrupted, with the followers of Judaism and Christianity going astray. The peoples that lived before Muhammad were forced to live under a corrupt religious system that failed to teach Islamic law and the five pillars of Islam. Devout peoples were led astray by Judaism and Christianity and could not please Allāh by obeying His commandments because His commandments had been lost, distorted and corrupted by the Christians and the Jews. It was not until Muhammad was sent as the seal of the Prophets to reveal the Qur'ān, which would be forever preserved without further corruption, that true worship of Allāh could be reinstituted in the world. One can thus make the same criticism that Dr. Bilal makes about Christianity about Islam: those who came before Muhammad were deprived of the purpose of creation.

C. The Purpose of Creation is to Test Human Conduct

Dr. Philips writes that the purpose of creation is to test human conduct (p. 50):

[T]he purpose for the creation of human beings in this world is to test their conduct. This world of life and death, wealth and poverty, sickness and health, was created to sift out the righteous souls from the evil souls. Human conduct in this world is the measure of faith.

It should be noted, however, that the tests of conduct are not to inform God about humankind, for He knew everything there was to know about them before he created them. The tests serve to confirm on the day of Judgment that those going to hell deserve it and those going to paradise only got there by God's grace. With regard to human beings in this life, the test of conduct serves two basic purposes: one, human spiritual growth, and the other, punishment or reward.

If this characterization is correct, then Dr. Philips paints a portrait of a cruel and arbitrary deity who creates human beings with full foreknowledge that they will sin and will thus consequently be cast into eternal damnation. All of this creation is created for the sole purpose of testing human conduct and sifting out the righteous from the evil. Yet the tests are not to inform God about humankind; God knew from the moment that every soul was created that it would turn to evil and deserved to go to hell for eternal damnation. Yet God, in his grace, chose to spare some of the souls from this eternal damnation (p. 50):

> The tests serve to confirm on the day of Judgment that those going to hell deserve it and those going to paradise only got there by God's grace.

And so we can state that God created creation with knowledge that every person that was created deserved hell. Through God's grace, some of the souls deserving death were spared eternal punishment, though Dr. Philips does not inform us of the precise reasons for why some are arbitrarily saved and yet others are punished. What we do, however, know is that all deserve punishment and God knew this at the time of creation. This hardly seems to be a just purpose for the creation of the world.

CHAPTER 6. SOME VALID BIBLICAL CRITICISMS

In the interests of fairness and impartiality, credit must be given to the proselytes of Islam where it is due. There are in fact some Scriptures that would appear to contradict themselves to an outsider not versed in biblical interpretation. Many of these can be explained through facts, circumstances or context, as we do below.

References to page numbers in this section refer to Dr. Baagil's *Muslim Christian Dialogue*.

I. Addition of Mark 16:9-20

Dr. Baagil writes that "The gospel of resurrection in Mark 16:9-20 has also been removed in many Bibles" (p. 39). This statement is part true, but generally false. I am unaware of any Bible that does not include Mark 16:9-20. The Revised Standard Version, which is cited by the author (p. 39), as well as the American Standard Version, Bible in Basic English, International Standard Version and King James Version, all include Mark 16:9-20. The English Standard Version contains the text in brackets. The NIV includes a brief note stating, "The earliest manuscripts and some other ancient witnesses do not have Mark 16:9-20." I have therefore found no evidence to suggest that Mark 16:9-20 "has also been removed in many Bibles" (p. 39).

However, it is true that some manuscripts do not contain Mark 16:9-20. It is therefore unclear whether the original manuscripts contains these verses or whether they were later additions. Many scholars believe they were included in the first manuscripts, but through age, the last part of Mark deteriorated. Thus, some later manuscripts did not copy the section. However, the church, based on some manuscripts, added the disputed sections back into later manuscripts.

A second flaw in Dr. Baagil's statement is his use of "resurrection" in his statement, "The gospel of resurrection in Mark 16:9-20 has also been removed in many Bibles" (p. 39). Dr. Baagil implies that the "resurrection" discussed in Mark was removed in some Bibles. This is a flawed reading. Even if Mark 16:9-20 were removed in some Bibles, a claim which is disputed above, the resurrection discussed in Mark would remain. When Mary Magdalene, Mary the mother of James, and Salome came to Jesus' tomb, an angel declared to them "You seek Jesus of Nazareth, who was crucified. He is risen!" (Mark 16:6). The passage "removed" in Mark 16:12 (Jesus "appeared in another form to two of them as they walked and went into the country") and Mark 16:14 (Jesus "appeared to the eleven as they sat at the table") are not necessary as the resurrection was already stated in Mark 16:6 ("He is risen!"). Therefore, whether or not the disputed verses were in the original Gospel is immaterial to whether the resurrection was preached in Mark.

II. Seeming Contradictions in Historical Narration

Examples of these seeming contradictions, followed by their explanations, are as follow:

A. Horsemen Taken by David

2Sa 8:4 David took from him one thousand chariots, **seven hundred horsemen**, and twenty thousand foot soldiers. Also David hamstrung all the chariot horses, except that he spared enough of them for one hundred chariots.	1Ch 18:4 David took from him one thousand chariots, **seven thousand horsemen**, and twenty thousand foot soldiers. Also David hamstrung all the chariot horses, except that he spared enough of them for one hundred chariots.

Possible explanation: An explanation offered by Gerardus D. Bouw in *The Book of Bible Problems*. He says on page 84: "Apparently the 6,300 were captured as a group while the remaining 700 were captured at a different time. In support of this theory he notes the differences in the language used in the two sections.

In II Samuel 8:3 it says David smote Hadadezer as he went *to recover* his border at the river Euphrates, while in I Chronicles 18:3 it says David smote Hadarezer as he went *to establish* his dominion by the river Euphrates.

So, in effect he is suggesting that Hadarezar initially went to stabilize his control over the Euphrates and David took his troops of 700 horsemen. Then Hadarezar sent another 6300 to recover his previous dominion and then these too were taken by David, thus making a total of 7,000.

B. Charioteers Killed by David

2Sa 10:18 Then the Syrians fled before Israel; and David killed **seven hundred charioteers** and **forty thousand horsemen** of the Syrians, and struck **Shobach** the commander of their army, who died there.	1Ch 19:18 Then the Syrians fled before Israel; and David killed **seven thousand charioteers** and **forty thousand foot soldiers** of the Syrians, and killed **Shophach** the commander of the army.

Regarding the 700 charioteers:

It is possible that 2 Samuel refers to the men in 700 chariots and 1 Chronicles refers to 7,000 men in chariots (*i.e.*, there were about 10 men in each chariot). However, this interpretation is not supported by the text.

Regarding the 40,000 horsemen / foot solders:

It is entirely conceivable that the 40,000 horsemen were also foot soldiers.

C. Whether Michal had Children

2Sa 6:23 Therefore Michal the daughter of Saul had no children to the day of her death.	2Sa 21:8 So the king took Armoni and Mephibosheth, the two sons of Rizpah the daughter of Aiah, whom she bore to Saul, and the five sons of Michal the daughter of Saul, whom she brought up for Adriel the son of Barzillai the Meholathite.

This can be explained by an error in some translations. Although the KJV, MKJV and NKJV refer to "Michal the daughter of Saul" in 2Sa 21:8, the ISV, NIV and many other editions refer to the five sons of "Merab," the daughter of Saul, whom she had borne to Adriel, who was her husband according to 1Sa 18:19. It would not make sense that 2Sa 21:8 refer to Michal because she was *not* Adriel's wife.

The reason why some translations, including the KJV, refer to Michael rather than Merab in 2Sa 21:8, is that the Septuagint (the Greek translation of the Hebrew) as well as all but two Hebrew manuscripts, refer to "Michal." However, it would appear that "Merab" was referenced in the original, since she was Adriel's wife. The reference to "Michael" is most likely an ancient scribal error.[19]

In either case, even if it was "Michal" referred to in 2Sa 21:8, the verse states that the five sons were "brought up for Adriel." It is thus possible that they were only her "sons" in a "surrogate" rather than biological sense.

D. Man's Days Limited to 120 Years

Gen 6:3 And the LORD said, "My Spirit shall not strive with man forever, for he is indeed flesh; yet his days shall be **one hundred and twenty years**."	This is not referring to our ages; otherwise, we would all live to be exactly 120 years old. Rather, it is referring to the amount of time left before the flood.
Gen 9:29 So all the days of Noah were nine hundred and fifty years; and he died.	The proper way to interpret this is understand 120 years as being the amount of time left between when God declared that man's years would be 120 (Gen 6:3) and the year the floods came (Gen 7:10-11).
Gen 11:11 After he begot Arphaxad, Shem lived **five hundred years**, and begot sons and daughters.	Noah was 500 years old when he begat Shem, Ham and Japheth (Gen 5:32) and 600 years old when the floods came (Gen 6:7:11). Therefore, in order for there to have been 120 years between when God declared that the floods would come and when they came, God must have declared the Gen 6:3 limit 20 years *before* Noah begat his sons. This would seem to be contradictory, since God's

	declaration in Gen 6:3 came after the begetting of Noah's sons in Gen 5:32. However, we should not read Genesis 5-6 as being chronological. We see several accounts in which accounts superimpose one another. One example are the varying creation accounts of Genesis 1 and Genesis 2.

E. Seeing God

John 5:37 And the Father Himself, who sent Me, has testified of Me. You have neither heard His voice at any time, nor seen His form. John 5:38 But you do not have His word abiding in you, because whom He sent, Him you do not believe.	In John 5:37, Jesus is speaking to the Pharisees, who do not hear God's voice nor see God because they do not believe Jesus, whom God sent. However, in John 14:9, to Philip the disciple, who believed, Jesus said he who has seen Jesus has seen the Father.
John 14:9 Jesus said to him, "Have I been with you so long, and yet you have not known Me, Philip? He who has seen Me has seen the Father; so how can you say, 'Show us the Father'?	To properly understand this, one should read Isaiah 6:9, which distinguishes between seeing and perceiving: "Keep on hearing, but do not understand; Keep on seeing, but do not perceive" ("do not see" in the NIV) or Luke 8:10, where Jesus references the Scripture in Isaiah, stating, "To you [the disciples] it has been given to know the mysteries of the kingdom of God, but to the rest it is given in parables, that 'seeing they may not see, and hearing they may not understand."

[19] See http://carm.org/bible-difficulties/joshua-esther/did-michal-have-any-children-or-not.

	Both the Pharisees and the disciples saw Jesus, but only the disciples believed and were thus able to see the Father.

F. Conclusion

On the one hand, one can argue that these points are irrelevant because they do not teach anything doctrinally essential. Whether 700 or 7,000 men were lost in battle is immaterial. On the other hand, these errors are significant because they may prove that the Bible that we have today is not error-free. If the Bible can have errors with respect to history, it is then entirely possible that it have errors with respect to larger doctrinal questions. However, as discussed above, there are various ways to explain the discrepancies that exist in various versions and translations of the Bible.

CHAPTER 7. PRAYER AND BENEDICTION OVER THE MUSLIM READER

To the Muslim who has received and read this book, I pray this prayer over you:

- I pray that you shall experience the living God and His one and only Son, Jesus Christ, through an encounter so real that you will be left knowing the divinity of Jesus and the truth of His Word in the Holy Bible;
- In this encounter with God, you will experience His love, a thing too great to describe in words, but that will leave you in awe;
- I pray that after knowing Jesus's divinity and experiencing His healing love, you will commit your life to following Him, even though it may cost you your life;
- In this way, you will both know and follow Jesus, the Son of God, and I will see you in heaven, and we shall rejoice.

Glossary

Kedar Second son of Ishmael, following Nebajoth (Gen 25:13; 1Ch 1:29). Also refers to a place in Arabia (see NIV Study Bible note on Psalm 120:5, at p. 922). Referenced in Isaiah 42:11 ("Let the wilderness and its cities lift up their voice, The villages that Kedar inhabits. Let the inhabitants of Sela sing, Let them shout from the top of the mountains").

Sela Referenced in Isaiah 42:11 ("Let the wilderness and its cities lift up their voice, The villages that Kedar inhabits. Let the inhabitants of Sela sing, Let them shout from the top of the mountains"). According to Ghada Khafagy, it is "a mountain in the city of Madina where Prophet Muhammad is buried" (*Where Hearts and Souls Meet*).

Valley of Baca Referenced in Psalm 84:4-6: "Blessed are those who dwell in Your house; They will still be praising You. Selah. Blessed is the man whose strength is in You, Whose heart is set on pilgrimage. As they pass through the Valley of Baca, They make it a spring; The rain also covers it with pools." According to the NIV Study Bible, *Baca* means either "weeping" or "balsam trees" common in arid valleys. "The place is unknown and may be figurative (see 23:4) for arid stretches the pilgrims had to traverse" (p. 875).

Zion A place name used synonymously as Jerusalem in the Bible. It commonly referred to a specific mountain near Jerusalem—Mount Zion—on which stood a Jebusite fortress of the same name that was conquered by David and later named the City of David.

www.ingramcontent.com/pod-product-compliance
Lightning Source LLC
La Vergne TN
LVHW051404080426
835508LV00022B/2970